Collins

Children's PICTURE ATLAS

Contents

How to use the atlas

Take a journey around the world with this atlas. It is divided up into continents, regions and countries. Each map is full of small picture symbols which will introduce you to the lifestyle of people, wildlife and interesting places found in far off lands.

World maps

The introductory pages show maps of the whole world and from these you can find the regions with the most interesting features. You can find out more about these by searching through the continents and regions mapped in the rest of the atlas. At the bottom of each World page is a list of symbols used on pages within the atlas. Try to find the countries where the symbols are shown then look at the other interesting features found in that country.

Below the world map each 'Did you know? lists some fascinating facts and statistics.

- Only 12 people have ever walked on the moon.
- It takes 45 minutes to put on a space suit.
- A spacecraft takes 3 days to travel from earth to the moon.

World

The world is full of interesting places. Many countries have famous buildings like castles, churches and palaces and some of these are named on the map.

Arctic

NORTH AMERICA

Seattle Space Needle

Statue of Liberty

Edinburgh Castle

EUROPE

Eiffel Tower

Colosseum

Kennedy Space Center

Atlantic Ocean

Mexican pyramid

Pacific Ocean

SOUTH AMERICA

Did you know?

- Only 12 people have ever walked on the moon.
- It takes 45 minutes to put on a space suit.
- A spacecraft takes 3 days to travel from earth to the moon.

Statue de Jesus

Did you know?

- The Eiffel tower is over 300 metres (984 feet) high.
- There are 1660 steps from the foot of the tower to the top.
- More than 2½ million rivets hold the tower together.
- In summer, the tower is 15 centimetres (6 inches) taller because of the warmer weather.

Look through the maps in this atlas to find the other places shown below.
▼

Arc de Triomphe

Golden Temple, Amritsar

terracotta soldier

Dome of the Rock

vi

Maps of each continent

How well do you know the flags of the world? Turn to the map of a continent and every flag will be shown beside its country. In addition all the statistics about the continent are listed. These include its highest mountain, longest river, biggest country and much more.

On every spread of a continent there is also a short activity which relates to the information shown on the map.

Atlanta

New Orleans

ST KITTS AND NEVIS

ANTIGUA AND BARBUDA

THE BAHAMAS
Nassau

Miami

DOMINICA

Gulf of Mexico

Havana

San Juan

CUBA

DOMINICAN REPUBLIC

BARBADOS

HAITI
Port-au-Prince

Santo Domingo

PUERTO RICO (USA)

Kingston

JAMAICA

Caribbean Sea

BELIZE

Belmopan

HONDURAS

GUATEMALA
Guatemala City

Tegucigalpa

ST LUCIA

GRENADA

Managua

Maps of regions and countries

Imagine you have just arrived in a new country. What will it be like? What do you want to do or see here?

The symbols placed on the countries can help you to decide. Look at the symbols in the neighbouring countries and plan a journey right across the region. There is so much to see and do.

Watch a Sumo wrestling match!
Take a train journey!

Go walking in the mountains!
See lots of animals!

Find out more from the facts placed around the maps.

It's a fact

The giant panda has lived in bamboo forests for several million years. Each year a panda can eat 5 tonnes of bamboo. There are only about 1600 left in the wild.

It's a fact

Ice hockey is one of Canada's most popular sports. It was first played in 1788 when some schoolboys tried to play the Irish game 'hurley' on ice. In Canada today there are over 500 000 players.

Try the activity found at the bottom of each map.

This will let you know just how much you have learnt from the map. All the answers are listed at the back of the atlas.

Try this!
China has many different animals. Look at the map and find

The big furry animal who loves to eat bamboo.

Many sports are played in Japan

Can you name 2 of these?

Try this!
Canada has many different animals and birds. Look at the map and find

4 types of bird
2 types of dog
3 furry wild animals

Where have you been?

You may like to see what other children think of the places they have visited or lived in. On pages 48–51 you can read some of the comments we have gathered from children. Have you been to the same places? What comment would you make about the places you have visited?

Kenya
We were in a big car and saw elephants and lions. I liked the lions but they had big teeth. It was very dusty and hot.
Katie

USA
I like Universal Studio because it has fantastic rides. I would give it a ten out of ten.
Sam

Index

You may know the name of a place you would like to visit but can't find the map it appears on. Turn to the index and find the name. The index will tell you which page in the atlas to turn to and where the place is on the map.

World

The world is full of interesting places. Many countries have famous buildings like castles, churches and palaces and some of these are named on the map.

Arctic

NORTH AMERICA

Seattle Space Needle

Statue of Liberty

Kennedy Space Center

Edinburgh Castle

EUROPE

Eiffel Tower

Colosseum

Mexican pyramid

Atlantic

Ocean

Pacific

Ocean

SOUTH AMERICA

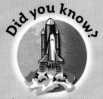

Did you know?

- Only 12 people have ever walked on the moon.
- It takes 45 minutes to put on a space suit.
- A spacecraft takes 3 days to travel from earth to the moon.

Statue de Jesus

Did you know?

- The Eiffel tower is over 300 metres (984 feet) high.
- There are 1660 steps from the foot of the tower to the top.
- More than 2½ million rivets hold the tower together.
- In summer, the tower is 15 centimetres (6 inches) taller because of the warmer weather.

Look through the maps in this atlas to find the other places shown below.

Arc de Triomphe

Golden Temple, Amritsar

terracotta soldier

Dome of the Rock

Interesting places

a n

Kremlin

A S I A

Great Wall of China

Pacific

Ocean

Taj Mahal

Sphinx

I C A

Indian

Ocean

Did you know?

- The Great Wall of China is the longest wall in the world.
- It winds up and down mountains and across fields and deserts.
- The wall is as tall as 2 double decker buses.

O C E A N I A

lu house

Sydney Opera House

Chilean chapel

Big Ben

Berber architecture

Angkor Wat

World

Animals and birds live all over the world. Each have their favourite places to live. This may depend on the climate and vegetation of the country in which they are found.

A r c t i

NORTH AMERICA

caribou

bobcat

bald eagle

gila monster

Highland cattle

EURO

puffin

camel

Atlantic

Ocean

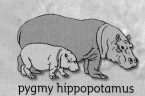

pygmy hippopotamus

jaguar

Pacific

Ocean

SOUTH AMERICA

Did you know?

- Penguins are birds that cannot fly.
- They have waterproof feathers and are expert swimmers.
- The smallest penguin is called a Fairy Penguin.

alpaca

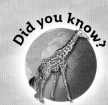

Did you know?

- The giraffe is the tallest animal in the world. It can grow to more than 5 metres (16 feet) tall.
- A giraffe can live without water for longer than a camel. It can run faster than a horse.
- A giraffe can clean its ears with its very long tongue.

Look through the maps in this atlas to find the other animals and birds shown below.
▼

penguins

koala

poison arrow frog

spiny anteater

peacock

Animals and Birds

lynx

brown bear

Siberian tiger

ASIA

Pacific

Ocean

raffe

gorilla

giant panda

Indian

Ocean

RICA

zebra

Did you know?

- A panda is a type of bear. It can climb trees.
- A baby panda is smaller than a mouse. When it is born, it cannot see.
- Pandas eat for up to 16 hours every day.

OCEANIA

kangaroo

kiwi

alligator

skunk

yak

snow goose

World

Different types of food are grown and eaten all over the world. This map of the world shows where some of our favourite foods are grown.

A r c t i c

N O R T H A M E R I C A

apples

peanuts

cranberries

hamburgers

cheese

EUROPE

pizza

dates

Atlantic

Ocean

bananas

oranges

Pacific

Ocean

S O U T H

A M E R I C A

Did you know?

- Apples can be all shades of red, green or yellow.
- One apple tree can produce 400 apples every year.
- Apples can be as small as a cherry, or as large as a grapefruit.

grapes

Did you know?

- A coconut can float on the water.
- Coconuts are grown in more than 90 countries of the world.
- You can drink coconut juice. It is the liquid found inside a coconut.

Look through the maps in this atlas to find the other foods shown below.
▼

tortilla

pumpkin pie

croissants

almonds

Food and Drink

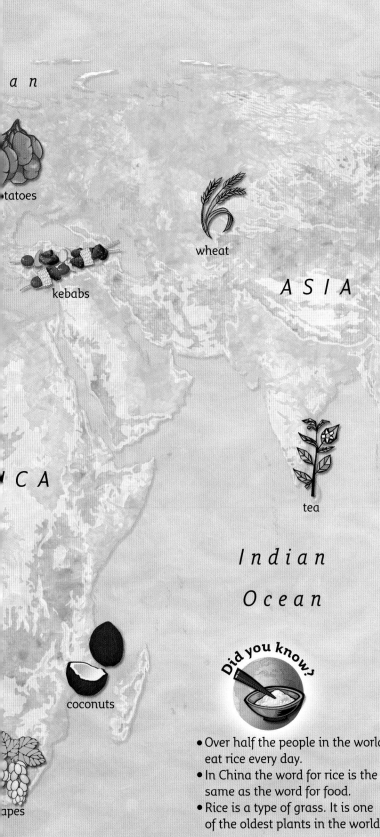

a n

tatoes

kebabs

wheat

A S I A

Pacific

Ocean

bowl of rice

tea

pineapples

Indian

Ocean

C A

coconuts

apes

Did you know?

- Over half the people in the world eat rice every day.
- In China the word for rice is the same as the word for food.
- Rice is a type of grass. It is one of the oldest plants in the world.

seafood

O C E A N I A

kiwi fruit

spaghetti

olives

wheat

sardines

World

People play sport all over the world. Popular sports, like football, are played in almost every country. Different sports are shown on the map.

Arctic

NORTH AMERICA

snow boarding

ice hockey

American football

football

cricket

EUROPE

bull fighting

rugby

Atlantic Ocean

Pacific Ocean

SOUTH AMERICA

surfing

football

Did you know?

- There are different types of football, such as American football, Australian football and Gaelic football.
- Blind people use a ball filled with ball bearings, so that they can hear it.
- Bright orange footballs are used when it is snowy.

motor racing

football

Did you know?

- Hockey can be played on ice, on a field or under the water.
- A hockey stick can be shaped like a J or an L.
- Hockey was played in Egypt thousands of years ago.

polo

Look through the maps in this atlas to find the other sports and activities shown below.
▼

curling

baseball

skiing

yachting

Sports and Activities

a n

chess

A S I A

Pacific

Ocean

karate

cricket

hockey

R I C A

Indian

Ocean

Did you know?

- To surf you stand or lie on a board and float on the waves of the sea.
- Dolphins and whales like to surf the waves.
- The word surf can also mean to look at different pages of the World Wide Web on a computer.

Australian football

tennis

O C E A N I A

icket

surfing

rugby

sumo wrestling

lacrosse

scuba diving

gymnastics

World

Seas and oceans cover two thirds of the earth's surface. The rest is land. The land is divided up into seven large masses of land known as continents.

Greenland

A r c t i c

Mount McKinley

Rocky Mountains

NORTH AMERICA

EURO

Atlas Mountains

Saha
Dese

R. Missouri

R. Mississippi

Niagara Falls

Yosemite Falls

The map shows some of the largest features on each continent.

Caribbean Sea

Atlantic

Ocean

Pacific

Ocean

Andes

Angel Falls

R. Amazon

SOUTH AMERICA

Andes

Did you know?

- Deserts cover a third of the world's surface.
- The Sahara is the world's largest desert.
- The highest sand dunes are found in Algeria.
- The highest temperatures in the world occur in the Sahara, however the nights can be very cold.

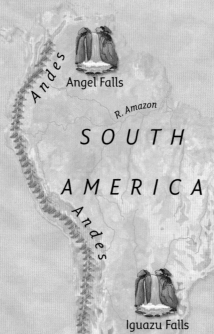

Did you know?

- The world's highest mountain range is Himalaya.
- Mount Everest is the highest peak at 8848 metres (29 029 feet).
- It was once known as Peak 15.
- Mount Everest was formed about 60 million years ago.
- Mount Everest was named after Sir George Everest the British surveyor-general of India.

*Na
De*

Iguazu Falls

Aconcagua

A global view of each continent is shown here. ▶

North America lies between the Atlantic and Pacific Oceans.

South America stretches from the Caribbean Sea towards the South Pole.

Europe is one of the smallest continents.

Natural Features

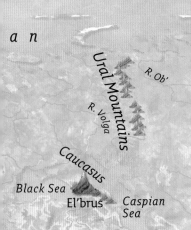

a n

Ural Mountains

R. Ob'

R. Volga

S i b e r i a

Caucasus

Black Sea

El'brus

Caspian Sea

ranean Sea

A S I A

Kunlun Shan

H i m a l a y a

R. Ganges

Mount Everest

Gobi Desert

Chang Jiang

Pacific Ocean

R. Nile

Arabian

Peninsula

Arabian Sea

Bay of Bengal

South China Sea

RICA

R. Congo

Kilimanjaro

Indian Ocean

Borneo

Puncak Jaya

New Guinea

ria Falls

Kalahari Desert

Tugela Falls

Did you know?

- Angel Falls, in Venezuela, is the world's highest waterfall at 979 metres (3212 feet).
- Victoria Falls, on the Zambezi river between Zambia and Zimbabwe, is the largest. It is 1.7 kilometres (1 mile) wide and 128 metres (420 feet) high.
- Niagara Falls is the most powerful falls in North America.

Great Sandy Desert

Great Victoria Desert

O C E A N I A

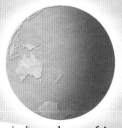

rica is almost equally balanced either side of the Equator.

Asia is the largest continent.

Oceania is made up of Australia and many small islands.

Antarctica encircles the South Pole.

World

Continents are divided up into many different countries. There are over 190 countries in the world. Lines are drawn on the map to show where two countries meet. These are known as international boundaries.

GREENLAND
(Denmark)

U.S.A.

CANADA

UNITED STATES OF AMERICA

More detailed map Europe can be found pages 22–29

Azores
(Portugal)

MOROCCO

TUNI

ALGERIA   LIB

WESTERN SAHARA

MEXICO

THE BAHAMAS

CUBA

HAITI   DOMINICAN REP.

MAURITANIA

MALI   NIGER

Mexico City ○
is the largest city
in North America

BELIZE   JAMAICA

PUERTO RICO
(USA)

CAPE VERDE   SENEGAL

THE GAMBIA

BURKINA

GUATEMALA   HONDURAS

EL SALVADOR   NICARAGUA

GUINEA-BISSAU   GUINEA

SIERRA LEONE

CÔTE D'IVOIRE

BENIN
TOGO
GHANA

NIGERIA

COSTA RICA

TRINIDAD & TOBAGO

LIBERIA

This map also shows the largest city in each continent. ○

PANAMA

VENEZUELA

GUYANA

SURINAME

FRENCH GUIANA

CAMEROON
EQUITORIAL GUINEA

COLOMBIA

GABON

Galapagos Is
(Ecuador)

ECUADOR

P E R U

B R A Z I L

ANC

Did you know?

BOLIVIA

PARAGUAY

Sao Paulo ○
is the largest city in
South America

NA

When it is 12 noon in New York the time is
• 5 pm in London
• 3 am in Sydney
• 8 pm in Moscow
• Midnight in Bangkok
• 9 am in Los Angeles

C H I L E

A R G E N T I N A

URUGUAY

Did you know?

These countries have two capital cities.
• The Netherlands has The Hague and Amsterdam
• Malaysia has Kuala Lumpur and Putrajaya
• Bolivia has La Paz and Sucre
• South Africa has Pretoria and Cape Town
• Myanmar has Naypyidaw and Yangon

The flags of the eight largest countries in the world are shown below. Look through the rest of the atlas to find out more interesting facts about life in these countries.

Falkland Islands
(UK)

South Georgia
(UK)

▼

Russian Federation	Canada	China	United States of America
17 075 400 square kilometres	9 984 670 square kilometres	9 620 671 square kilometres	9 826 635 square kilometre
6 592 849 square miles	3 855 103 square miles	3 714 562 square miles	3 794 085 square miles

Countries and Cities

RUSSIAN FEDERATION

○ **Moscow**
is the largest city
in Europe

KAZAKHSTAN

MONGOLIA

GEORGIA
ARMENIA AZERBAIJAN
UZBEKISTAN
KYRGYZSTAN
TURKMENISTAN
TAJIKISTAN

N. KOREA

JAPAN

○ **Tokyo**
is the largest city
in Asia

TURKEY

S. KOREA

YPRUS SYRIA
LEBANON
ISRAEL
JORDAN
IRAQ
KUWAIT
IRAN
AFGHAN-
ISTAN

PAKISTAN

CHINA

○
Cairo
the largest
ty in Africa
SAUDI
BAHRAIN
QATAR
UNITED ARAB
EMIRATES

NEPAL BHUTAN

EGYPT
ARABIA OMAN

INDIA
BANGLA-
DESH

MYANMAR
(BURMA)

LAOS
VIETNAM

ERITREA YEMEN
DJIBOUTI

THAILAND

PHILIPPINES

CAMBODIA

MARSHALL
ISLANDS

UDAN

SOUTH
SUDAN
ETHIOPIA
SOMALIA

SRI
LANKA

BRUNEI
MALAYSIA

Northern
Mariana Is.
(USA)

PALAU
FED. STATES OF
MICRONESIA

MALDIVES

UGANDA
CRATIC
LIC
RWANDA
KENYA
SINGAPORE

BURUNDI

SEYCHELLES

INDONESIA

NAURU

PAPUA
NEW
GUINEA

TANZANIA

SOLOMON
ISLANDS

COMOROS

EAST
TIMOR

MBIA
MALAWI
MOZAMBIQUE

MAURITIUS

VANUATU

FIJI

MBABWE
MADAGASCAR

New
Caledonia
(France)

VANA

Did you know?

AUSTRALIA

SWAZILAND

The time taken to fly between
● Los Angeles and Sydney is 14½ hours
● London and Tokyo is 12½ hours
● Paris and New York is 8½ hours
● Bangkok and Perth is 6¾ hours

LESOTHO

OF
TH
CA

○ **Sydney**
is the largest city
in Oceania

*Îles Kerguélen
(France)*

NEW
ZEALAND

Brazil	Australia	India	Argentina
8 514 879 square kilometres	7 692 024 square kilometres	3 064 989 square kilometres	2 766 889 square kilometres
3 287 613 square miles	2 969 907 square miles	1 183 364 square miles	1 068 302 square miles

North America

North America is the largest continent in the western hemisphere. It is surrounded by great oceans: the Arctic to the north, the Pacific to the west and the Atlantic to the east. The countries of North America are a mixture of the large nations of Canada, USA and Mexico in the north and the tiny Caribbean island nations in the south. It is joined to South America by the narrow strip of land known as the isthmus of Panama.

People facts

- Population: 517 000 000
- Country with most people: United States of America 298 213 000
- City with most people: Mexico City 19 013 000

Geography facts

- Area: 24 680 331 square kilometres (9 529 129 square miles)
- Largest country: Canada 9 984 670 square kilometres (3 855 103 square miles)
- Longest river: Mississippi-Missouri 5969 kilometres (3709 miles)
- Highest mountain: Mount McKinley 6194 metres (20 321 feet)
- Largest lake: Lake Superior 82 100 square kilometres (31 698 square miles)
- Largest island: Greenland 2 175 600 square kilometres (840 004 square miles)

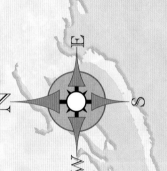

N
W   E
S

Arctic Ocean

GREENLAND
(Denmark)

Nuuk

Baffin Bay

Baffin Island

Hudson Bay

CANADA

Rocky

Bering Sea

ALASKA
U.S.A.

Mount
McKinley

Anchorage

Did you know?

- The United States has over 250 000 rivers.

- There are over 10 000 glaciers on Baffin Island.

- The world's smallest volcano is in Puebla, Mexico.

- Belize's barrier reef at 285 kilometres (180 miles) is the longest in the western hemisphere.

- Some of the world's oldest rocks are found on the west coast of Greenland.

- 2 million caribou live in Canada.

Try this!

Unscramble these letters to find an island name.

Clue: It is the largest island in North America.

G L D E A N R E N

Answers at the back of the atlas.

3

Canada

N W E S

polar bear

Arctic Ocean

U.S.A.
A L A S K A

volcanoes

walrus

Mount McKinley

R. Yukon

caribou

ice breaker ship

Arctic hare

Arctic terns

husky dog

Gulf of Alaska

brown bear

Mount Logan

wolves

musk ox

R o c k y

Arctic fox

moose

Pacific Ocean

forest

lumberjack

M o u n t a i n s

killer whale

Mount Waddington

skiing

oil

C A N A

ice hockey

blueberries

port

Vancouver

Calgary

bobcat

Canadian Pacific Railway

wheat growing

Winnipeg

lacros

Canada is a huge country but it is not crowded.
The far north of the country is in the Arctic region
and is almost empty. Further south there are pine
forests and in the west are the Rocky Mountains.

U N I T E D   S T A T E S
O F   A M E R I C A

⑤ ④ ③ ② ①

Ⓐ Ⓑ Ⓒ

polar bear

Greenland
(Denmark)

seal

igloo

Inuit people

Baffin Island

fishing

ptarmigan

Canadian goose

Nuuk
(Godthåb)

kayak

snowy owl

beluga whale

D A

udson Bay

maple leaf

beaver

Newfoundland dog

Atlantic Ocean

timber

maple syrup

R. St Lawrence

lobster

urling

erior

apples

apples

Ottawa church

Quebec

Montreal

Ottawa

cranberries

Toronto

Lake Ontario

Lake Michigan

Lake Huron

Lake Erie

Niagara Falls

D

E

Did you know?

- Canada has the world's longest coastline – 202 000 kilometres (125 517 miles).
- The Arctic hare has huge feet which help it to run on top of the snow.
- Canadians consume more macaroni and cheese than any other nation on earth.

What am I?

- I grow on a tree at the end of a twig.
- I am the national emblem of Canada.
- I can be seen as a bright red symbol on my country's national flag.
- Canadians eat the syrup which is taken from the trunk of my tree.

What am I?

Try this!

Canada has many different animals and birds. Look at the map and find

4 types of bird
2 types of dog
3 furry wild animals

Answers at the back of the atlas.

It's a fact

Ice hockey is one of Canada's most popular sports. It was first played in 1788 when some schoolboys tried to play the Irish game 'hurley' on ice. In Canada today there are over 500 000 players.

5

United States of America

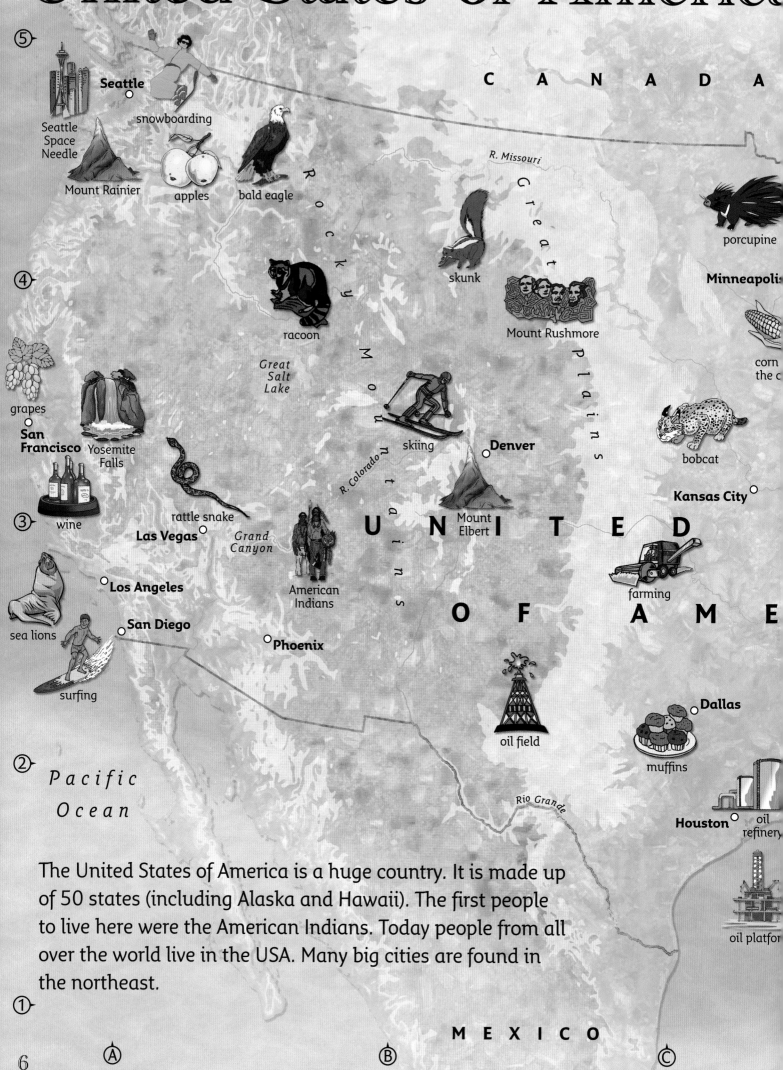

Seattle

snowboarding

Seattle
Space
Needle

Mount Rainier

apples

bald eagle

CANADA

R. Missouri

porcupine

④

skunk

Minneapolis

racoon

Mount Rushmore

corn
the c

Great
Salt
Lake

grapes

San
Francisco

Yosemite
Falls

skiing

Denver

bobcat

Kansas City

wine

③

rattle snake

Las Vegas

Grand
Canyon

Mount
Elbert

R. Colorado

UNITED

sea lions

Los Angeles

American
Indians

OF

AME

San Diego

farming

Phoenix

surfing

oil field

Dallas

muffins

②

Pacific

Ocean

Rio Grande

Houston

oil
refinery

The United States of America is a huge country. It is made up
of 50 states (including Alaska and Hawaii). The first people
to live here were the American Indians. Today people from all
over the world live in the USA. Many big cities are found in
the northeast.

oil platfor

①

MEXICO

Ⓐ

Ⓑ

Ⓒ

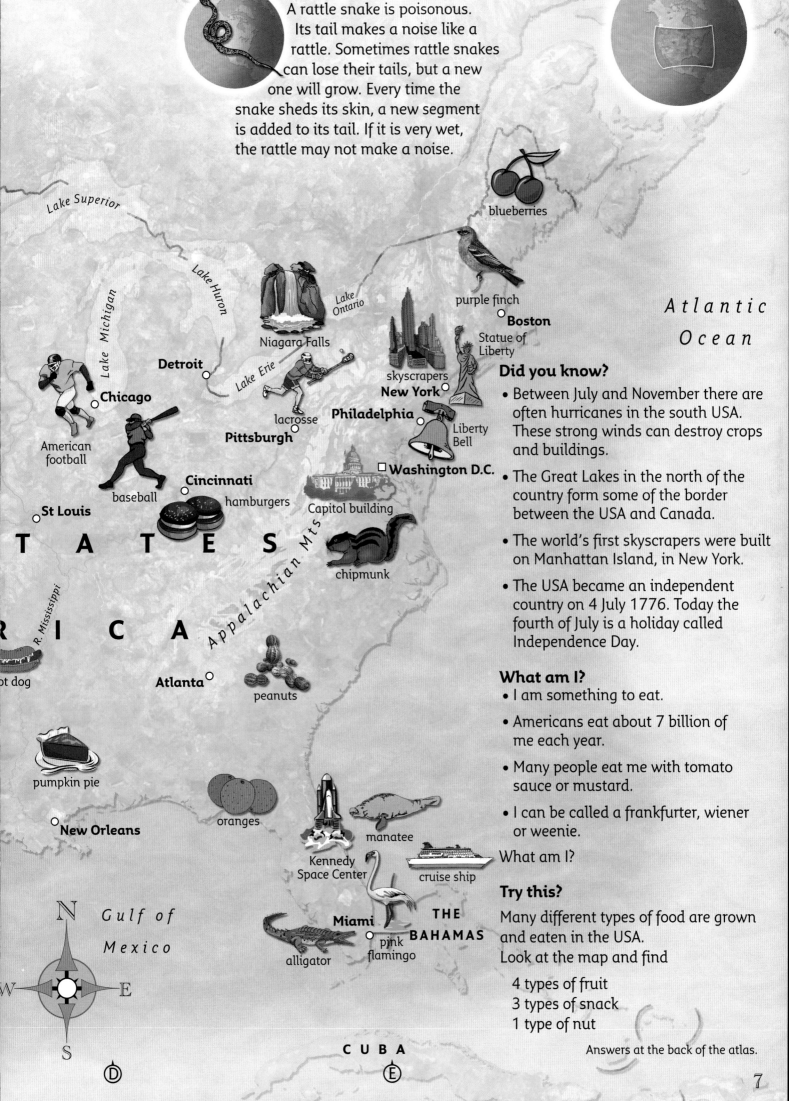

It's a fact

A rattle snake is poisonous. Its tail makes a noise like a rattle. Sometimes rattle snakes can lose their tails, but a new one will grow. Every time the snake sheds its skin, a new segment is added to its tail. If it is very wet, the rattle may not make a noise.

Lake Superior

blueberries

Lake Huron

Lake Michigan

Niagara Falls

Lake Ontario

purple finch

Boston

Statue of Liberty

Detroit

Lake Erie

skyscrapers

Atlantic Ocean

Chicago

lacrosse

New York

American football

Pittsburgh

Philadelphia

Liberty Bell

baseball

Cincinnati

hamburgers

☐ **Washington D.C.**

St Louis

Capitol building

T A T E S

chipmunk

R. Mississippi

R I C A

Appalachian Mts

ot dog

Atlanta

peanuts

pumpkin pie

oranges

New Orleans

Kennedy Space Center

manatee

cruise ship

N

Gulf of Mexico

Miami

pink flamingo

THE BAHAMAS

alligator

W

E

S

C U B A

Did you know?

- Between July and November there are often hurricanes in the south USA. These strong winds can destroy crops and buildings.

- The Great Lakes in the north of the country form some of the border between the USA and Canada.

- The world's first skyscrapers were built on Manhattan Island, in New York.

- The USA became an independent country on 4 July 1776. Today the fourth of July is a holiday called Independence Day.

What am I?
- I am something to eat.

- Americans eat about 7 billion of me each year.

- Many people eat me with tomato sauce or mustard.

- I can be called a frankfurter, wiener or weenie.

What am I?

Try this?

Many different types of food are grown and eaten in the USA.
Look at the map and find

4 types of fruit
3 types of snack
1 type of nut

Answers at the back of the atlas.

Mexico and the Caribbean

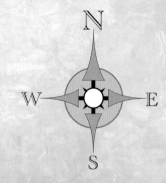

N
W · E
S

Tijuana

Ciudad Juárez

UNITED STATES OF AMERICA

Rio Grande

Gulf of California

Baja California

Sierra

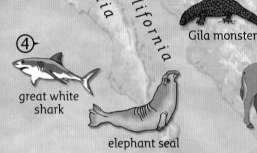
cactus

Gulf of Mexico

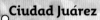
Gila monster

④

great white shark

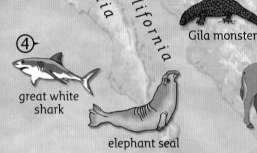
elephant seal

Torreón

donkey

Tabasco sauce

Monterrey

tortilla

M E X I C O

Madre

León

tacos

Guadalajara

football

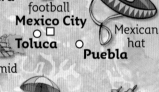
Mexico City

Toluca

Mexican hat

Puebla

Mexican pyramid

sun bathing

red chilli

Mexican temple

bull fighting

Yucatán

BELIZ

Belmopan

coral

GUATEMALA

Guatemala City

H O N

Tegucig

San Salvador

EL SALVADOR

Did you know?
- The country name Panama means 'place of many fish'.

③
- It took over 30 years to build the Panama canal.

- Around 35 species of lobster live in the Caribbean Sea.

- In Tobago, goat racing is one of the most popular sports.

What am I?
- I like to live in hot, dry places.

- I can live without rain for a long time.

②
- I do not have leaves and I am often spiny.

- I can hold lots of water.

- Sometimes I am grown as a houseplant.

What am I?

turtle

Try this!
Many different species of fish and birds are found in this region.
Look at the map and find

   6 types of fish and sea animals
①
   2 types of bird

P a c i f i c

O c e a n

Answers at the back of the atlas.

The land between the USA and South America is known as Central America. Mexico is the largest country here. There is dry desert in northern Mexico and wet rainforest in southern Central America. The Caribbean is the area to the east, where there are hundreds of tropical islands.

Bermuda

A t l a n t i c
O c e a n

cruise ship

□ **Nassau**

THE BAHAMAS

Turks and Caicos Islands

Havana □

CUBA

cigars

Monarch butterfly

sugar cane

mangoes

reggae singer

limes

DOMINICAN REPUBLIC

HAITI
Port-au-Prince □

Santo Domingo □

parrot

San Juan □

cruise ship

ST KITTS AND NEVIS

Anguilla

Cayman Is

uba ving

butterflies

JAMAICA

Kingston □

Rum

rum

gourds

bananas

PUERTO RICO

radio telescope

volcano

Montserrat
Guadeloupe

DOMINICA

Martinique

ST LUCIA

pineapples

ANTIGUA AND BARBUDA

C a r i b b e a n

S e a

sea horse

ST VINCENT AND THE GRENADINES

GRENADA

BARBADOS

bananas

ARAGUA

nagua

Lake Nicaragua

toucan

tropical fish

monk seal

Aruba

oil platform

yachting

TRINIDAD & TOBAGO

cricket

OSTA RICA
□ **San José**

Panama Canal

coffee

Panama City □
PANAMA

coconuts

V E N E Z U E L A

monkey

It's a fact

C O L O M B I A

Sea horses are a species of fish. They live in warm tropical waters. They eat slowly, sucking up food through their long noses. Sea horses can move their eyes all around, without moving their bodies. They wrap their long, curly tails around seaweed to stay in one place.

Ⓓ

Ⓔ

Ⓕ

South America

⑦ South America stretches farther south from the equator than all the other continents. The longest mountain range in the world, the Andes, runs the full length of the continent. The Amazon rainforest is the largest in the world. Colourful birds and butterflies, giant snakes, jaguars, monkeys and pumas can all be found in this lush forest. People speak

⑥ Portuguese in Brazil, but Spanish in other countries.

N
W   E
S

Atlantic Ocean

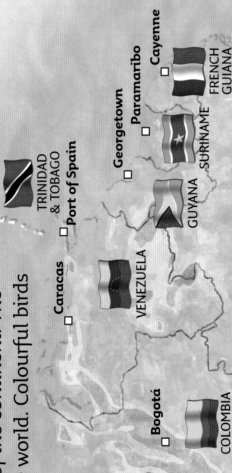

TRINIDAD & TOBAGO
Port of Spain

Cayenne

Paramaribo

FRENCH GUIANA

Georgetown

SURINAME

Caracas

VENEZUELA

GUYANA

Bogotá

COLOMBIA

Quito

ECUADOR

Galapagos Islands
(Ecuador)

Pacific Ocean

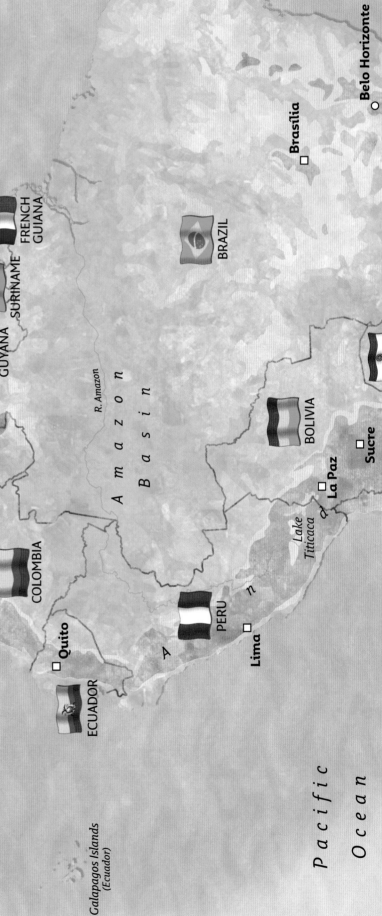

R. Amazon

A m a z o n   B a s i n

A n

A

PERU

Lima

Lake Titicaca

BRAZIL

Brasília

Belo Horizonte

BOLIVIA

La Paz

Sucre

⑤

São Paulo

Did you know?

- La Paz is the world's highest capital city.

- Columbia was named after Christopher Columbus.

- More than 2000 different species of butterflies are found in the rainforests of South America.

- Alpacas live in the mountains of Peru, Bolivia and Chile. They come in over 22 colours and do not like being touched.

- Ecuador is the world's leading exporter of bananas.

Asunción

Montevideo

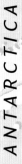

URUGUAY

Buenos Aires

ARGENTINA

South Georgia
(UK)

Falkland
Islands
(UK)

S

Aconcagua ▲

Tierra del
Fuego

Santiago

CHILE

ANTARCTICA

Southern Ocean

People facts

- Population: 375 000 000

- Country with most people: Brazil 186 405 000

- City with most people: São Paulo 18 333 000

③

Geography facts

- Area: 17 815 420 square kilometres (6 878 572 square miles)

- Largest country: Brazil 8 514 879 square kilometres (3 287 613 square miles)

- Longest river: Amazon 6516 kilometres (4049 miles)

- Highest mountain: Aconcagua 6959 metres (22 834 feet)

- Largest lake: Lake Titicaca 8340 square kilometres (3220 square miles)

- Largest island: Tierra del Fuego 47 000 square kilometres (18 147 square miles)

②

Try this!

Find 2 countries beginning with the letter C.

Find 2 capital cities beginning with the letter B.

Answers at the back of the atlas.

①

11

South America North

Most people in this area live on the low land near the coast. Ecuador is the Spanish word for equator. The equator is an imaginary line around the middle of the earth. Many unique species of animal live in the area. Potatoes, peppers and beans have been grown here for thousands of years.

Caribbean Sea

④

Barranquilla
Cartagena

Maracaibo
Barquisimeto
Valencia

Caracas

Port of Spai
TRINIDA
& TOBA

oil refineries

oil wells

PANAMA

Bucaramanga

iguana

puma

jaguar

R. Orinoco

VENEZUELA

GUYA

poisc
arrov
frog

Medellín

Angel Falls

Guiana

Bogotá

coffee

emeralds

③

Cali

COLOMBIA

R. Negro

sl

Quito

Mount Cotopaxi

ECUADOR

coffee

manta ray

Guayaquil

football

capybara

tapir

butterflies

Man

Amazon
Basin

②

condor

panpipes

monkeys

R. Madeira

anaconda

B

Pacific
Ocean

llama

PERU

rubber

deforestation

①

Lima

coffee

BOLIVIA

Ⓐ   Ⓑ   Ⓒ

N
W E
S

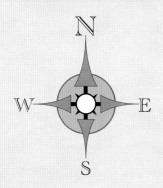

It's a fact

Andean panpipes are musical instruments made from pipes strapped together. The pipes are made from a reed called 'songo'. Songo grows on the banks of Lake Titicaca. Andean panpipes are also called zampoñas.

Did you know?

• The River Amazon carries more water than the rivers Nile, Chang Jiang and Mississippi combined.

• The Amazon is the largest rainforest in the world. About half of the world's plants, animals and insects are found there.

• The world's highest railway station, La Galera, is in Peru.

What am I?

• I live in the mountains and can reach more than 50 years of age.

• I can glide through the air for very long distances.

• Sometimes I eat so much that I can't get off the ground to fly.

• I am one of the world's largest vultures.

What am I?

Try this!

Look at the map and find

2 precious stones
1 deadly snake

Answers at the back of the atlas.

orgetown

Paramaribo

rocket launch

Cayenne

FRENCH GUIANA

URINAME

hlands

cayenne peppers

Atlantic Ocean

Belém

R. Amazon

Fortaleza

toucan

armadillo

sugar cane

Natal

R **A** **Z** **I** **L**

surfing

Recife

porcupines

R. Tocantins

R. São Francisco

Maceió

arrot

Brazilian Highlands

Ⓓ diamonds

Ⓔ

Salvador Ⓕ

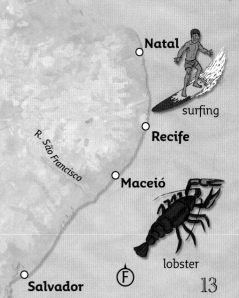

lobster

13

South America South

⑦ Running down the west coast of this area is the driest place on earth, the Atacama Desert. The southern tip of South America is very cold and there are icebergs in the sea. Many people in Paraguay are descended from the Indians who lived in South America before people from Europe arrived.

N
W — E
S

B r a z i l i a n

*Planalto do
Mato Grosso*

B R A Z I L

□ **Brasília**
○ **Goiânia**

coffee growing

Highlands

○ **Belo Horizonte**

beaches

Statue de Jesus ○ **Rio de Janeiro**

carnivals

Campinas
São Paulo ○
Santos ○

oranges

Curitiba ○

footballer

R. Paraná

Iguaçu Falls

□ **Asunción**
football

PARAGUAY

R. Paraguay

Chaco

Gran

R. Paraná

sheep

Argentinian church

R. Salado

A N

chinchilla

p

⑤

pelican

Chilean stag beetle

ᴇ

l

Desert

man in poncho

A t a c a m a

s

○ **Santa Cruz**

anteater

B O L I V I A

□ **Sucre**

La Paz □
skiing

Lake Titicaca

P E R U

alpaca

potatoes

⑥

Did you know?

• Chile is 10 times longer than it is wide.

• The sea around Cape Horn, south of

Spanish.

- Millions of sheep and cattle are farmed on the flat grassy plains known as the pampas. They are looked after by Gauchos, or cowboys.

- Almost all of Paraguay's electricity comes from hydroelectric power.

- Uruguay has won several Olympic medals for football.

What am I?

- I live in the sea.
- I am black and white and have a large fin.
- I am very sociable and have a good memory.
- I am noisy. I make lots of clicks and whistles.
- I have been around for millions of years.
- I can be called Orca.

What am I?

Try this!

Look at the map and find 2 types of fish

Many sports are played in South America Can you name 3 of these?

Answers at the back of the atlas.

It's a fact

Anteaters eat ants and termites. They have a long, sticky tongue and no teeth. Their front claws are strong and sharp. The babies ride on their mother's back.

URUGUAY

Córdoba

Rosario

Buenos Aires

Montevideo

Santiago

Mendoza

Rio de la Plata

R. Negro

Pacific Ocean

Atlantic Ocean

South Georgia (UK)

Falkland Islands (UK)

Tierra del Fuego

Cape Horn

PATAGONIA

oil tanker

sardines

mackerel

wine

polo

motor racing

tango dancers

wine

gaucho

vineyards

grapes

Chilean chapel

fishing boats

albatross

elephant seals

glaciers

penguins

puma

southern whale

killer whale

A B C D

① ② ③

15

Africa

Africa is the second largest continent. It is 3 times the area of Europe.

From the Mediterranean Sea in the north, Africa stretches approximately 8000 kilometres (4971 miles) to its most southerly point, Cape Agulhas. Most of northern Africa lies in and around the Sahara desert, while large areas of central Africa are covered in dense tropical rainforest.

People facts

- Population: 909 000 000
- Country with most people: Nigeria 131 530 000
- City with most people: Cairo 11 146 000

Geography facts

- Area: 30 343 578 square kilometres (11 715 721 square miles)
- Largest country: Algeria 2 381 741 square kilometres (919 595 square miles)
- Longest river: Nile 6695 kilometres (4160 miles)
- Highest mountain: Kilimanjaro 5892 metres (19 331 feet)
- Largest lake: Lake Victoria 68 800 square kilometres (26 563 square miles)
- Largest island: Madagascar 587 040 square kilometres (226 657 square miles)

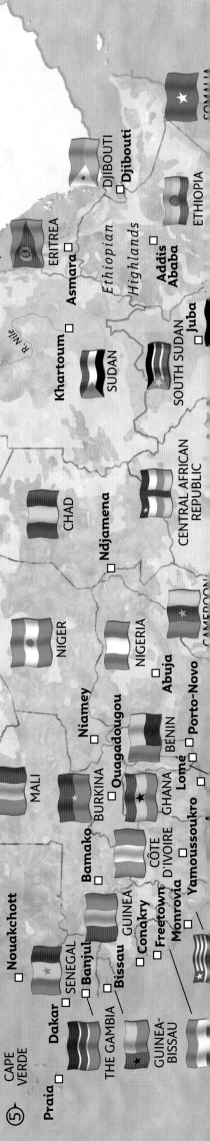

EUROPE

ASIA

Mediterranean Sea

Red Sea

Azores (Portugal)

Madeira (Portugal)

Canary Is (Spain)

Atlas Mountains

S a h a r a

Ethiopian Highlands

R. Nile

CAPE VERDE — Praia

SENEGAL — Dakar

THE GAMBIA — Banjul

GUINEA-BISSAU — Bissau

GUINEA — Conakry

SIERRA LEONE — Freetown

LIBERIA — Monrovia

MAURITANIA — Nouakchott

WESTERN SAHARA — Laayoune

MOROCCO — Rabat

ALGERIA — Algiers

TUNISIA — Tunis

LIBYA — Tripoli

EGYPT — Cairo

MALI — Bamako

BURKINA — Ouagadougou

CÔTE D'IVOIRE — Yamoussoukro

GHANA

BENIN — Porto-Novo

TOGO — Lomé

NIGER — Niamey

NIGERIA — Abuja

CHAD — Ndjamena

CENTRAL AFRICAN REPUBLIC

SUDAN — Khartoum

SOUTH SUDAN — Juba

ERITREA — Asmara

DJIBOUTI — Djibouti

ETHIOPIA — Addis Ababa

SOMALIA

CAMEROON

Map of Africa (southern and eastern)

SEYCHELLES
Victoria

MAURITIUS
Port Louis

Reunion (France)

COMOROS
□ **Moroni**

Mayotte (France)

Antananarivo □
MADAGASCAR

I n d i a n   O c e a n

KENYA
□ **Nairobi**
▲ *Kilimanjaro*

Lake Victoria

TANZANIA

RWANDA
□ **Kigali**

Bujumbura □
BURUNDI

Dodoma □

MALAWI
Lilongwe □

MOZAMBIQUE

Harare □
ZIMBABWE

Lusaka □
ZAMBIA

Maputo □

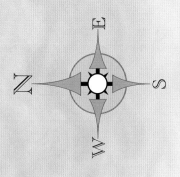
SWAZILAND

Pretoria (Tshwane) □
Mbabane □
Maseru □
LESOTHO

BOTSWANA
Gaborone □

REPUBLIC OF SOUTH AFRICA

Cape Agulhas

DEMOCRATIC REPUBLIC OF THE CONGO

Kinshasa □

CONGO
Brazzaville □

ANGOLA

Luanda □

GABON

NAMIBIA

Windhoek □

Cape Town □

TOGO

SÃO TOMÉ & PRÍNCIPE

EQUATORIAL GUINEA

Ascension Island (UK)

St Helena (UK)

A t l a n t i c   O c e a n

Did you know?

- The African elephant is the heaviest animal in the world.
- The Sahara Desert is the largest in the world and nearly as big as the whole of Europe.
- Mount Kenya is on the equator, but its peak is always covered in snow.
- About 400 languages are spoken in Nigeria.
- The Goliath beetle found near the equator in Africa is one of the largest insects in the world.
- In the rainforests of central Africa, it rains almost every day.
- The sea around the Cape of Good Hope is rough and dangerous. Gale force winds blow there most of the time.

Try this!

Unscramble these letters to find the country.
Clue: It is surrounded by sea.

C A R D A M S A G A

Answers at the back of the atlas.

N
E
S
W

A   B   C   D

① ② ③

17

Northern Africa

Did you know?

- There are over 500 tribes in Sudan. The tribes speak more than 100 different languages.

- Although there are many different languages, most people in northern Africa can speak Arabic.

- In Nigeria, twins are always called the same names. The first twin is called Taiwo. The second twin is called Kehinde.

- In Egypt, many people live on the banks of the River Nile, where they can grow food.

- Lake Chad is very shallow and is shrinking fast.

What am I?

- I am used for transport, milk, meat and wool.

- I can survive without water for about 2 weeks and without food for around a month.

- My thick coat reflects sunshine and my long eyelashes protect my eyes from sand.

- I can have one or two humps.

What am I?

Answers at the back of the atlas.

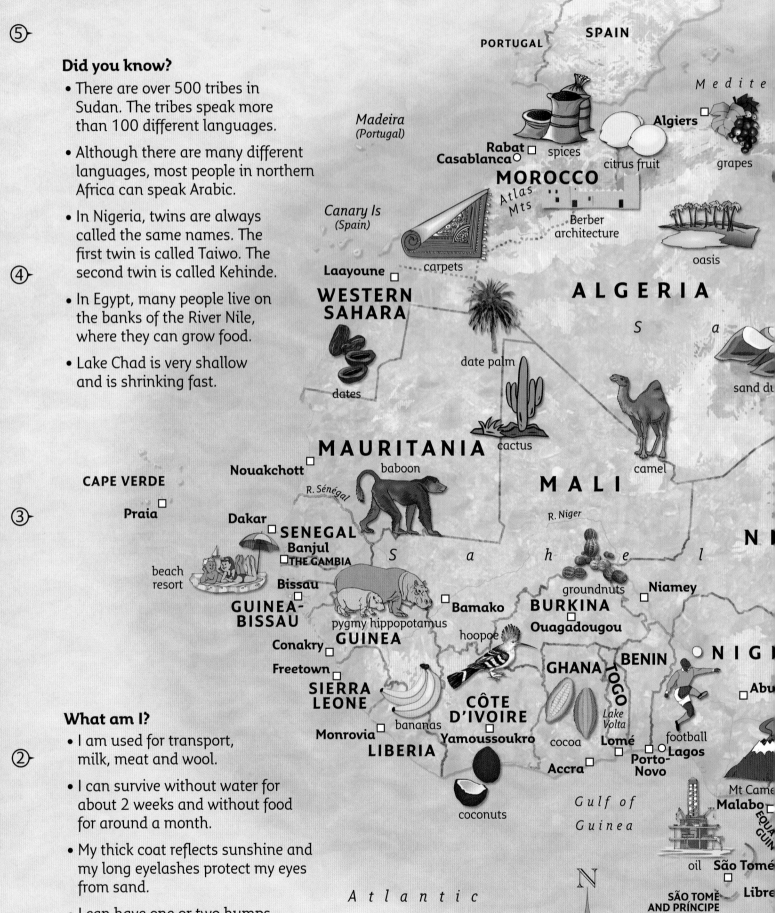

PORTUGAL
SPAIN

Medite

Madeira (Portugal)

Rabat
Casablanca
spices
Algiers
citrus fruit
grapes

MOROCCO

Atlas Mts
Berber architecture

Canary Is (Spain)

oasis

Laayoune
carpets

WESTERN SAHARA

ALGERIA

S   a

date palm

dates

sand du

MAURITANIA
cactus
camel

baboon

CAPE VERDE

Nouakchott

R. Sénégal

MALI

R. Niger

N

Praia

Dakar

SENEGAL

Banjul
THE GAMBIA

S   a   h   e   l

beach resort

Bissau

GUINEA-BISSAU

pygmy hippopotamus

Bamako

groundnuts

Niamey

BURKINA

Ouagadougou

Conakry

GUINEA

hoopoe

GHANA

BENIN

TOGO

N I G I

Freetown

SIERRA LEONE

CÔTE D'IVOIRE

Lake Volta

Abu

Monrovia

bananas

Yamoussoukro

LIBERIA

cocoa

Lomé

football

Lagos

Porto-Novo

Accra

Mt Came

Malabo

EQUA GUIN

coconuts

Gulf of Guinea

oil

São Tomé

Atlantic Ocean

SÃO TOMÉ AND PRÍNCIPE

Libre

N

W   E

S

Africa is connected to the continent of Asia at the narrow Sinai peninsula, north of the Red Sea. It is separated narrowly from Europe by the Strait of Gibraltar. Much of northern Africa is dry desert: the Sahara Desert and the Sahel region.

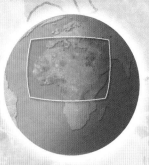

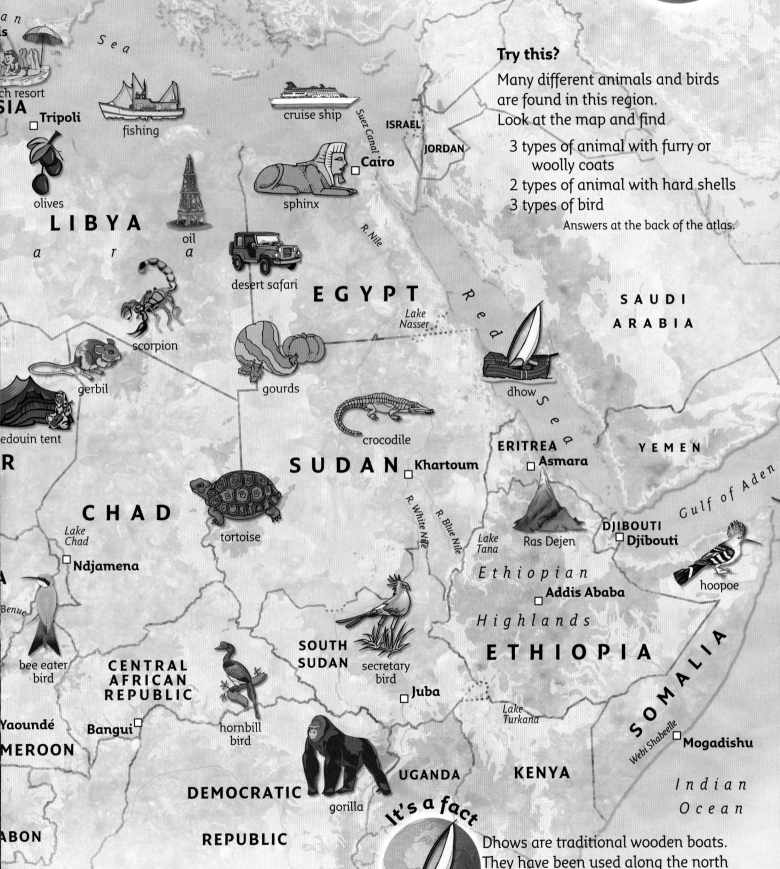

Sea

ch resort

Tripoli □

fishing

cruise ship

Suez Canal

ISRAEL

JORDAN

olives

L I B Y A

oil

a
r
a

sphinx

Cairo ●

R. Nile

E G Y P T

desert safari

Lake Nasser

S A U D I

A R A B I A

scorpion

gerbil

gourds

dhow

edouin tent

crocodile

Red

S U D A N ●**Khartoum**

□

ERITREA

□ **Asmara**

Sea

Y E M E N

Gulf of Aden

C H A D

Lake Chad

tortoise

DJIBOUTI

□ **Djibouti**

□ **Ndjamena**

R. White Nile

R. Blue Nile

Lake Tana

Ras Dejen

hoopoe

Benue

E t h i o p i a n

Addis Ababa □

bee eater bird

C E N T R A L

A F R I C A N

R E P U B L I C

SOUTH

SUDAN

secretary bird

H i g h l a n d s

E T H I O P I A

□ **Juba**

Lake Turkana

S
O
M
A
L
I
A

Yaoundé

Bangui □

hornbill bird

gorilla

Webi Shabeelle

□ **Mogadishu**

MEROON

UGANDA

KENYA

I n d i a n

O c e a n

DEMOCRATIC

gorilla

It's a fact

ABON

REPUBLIC

CONGO

OF THE CONGO

Dhows are traditional wooden boats. They have been used along the north and east coasts of Africa for thousands of years. Their triangular sails are called lateens. Dhows are used to transport people, animals, fish and other goods.

ANGOLA

Ⓓ

Ⓔ **TANZANIA**

Ⓕ

19

Try this?

Many different animals and birds are found in this region.
Look at the map and find

3 types of animal with furry or woolly coats

2 types of animal with hard shells

3 types of bird

Answers at the back of the atlas.

Southern Africa

⑦

At the centre of southern Africa is the huge rainforest of the River Congo and the Congo Basin. The Great Rift Valley is surrounded by some of the highest mountains in Africa. In the southwest are the Kalahari and Namib deserts.

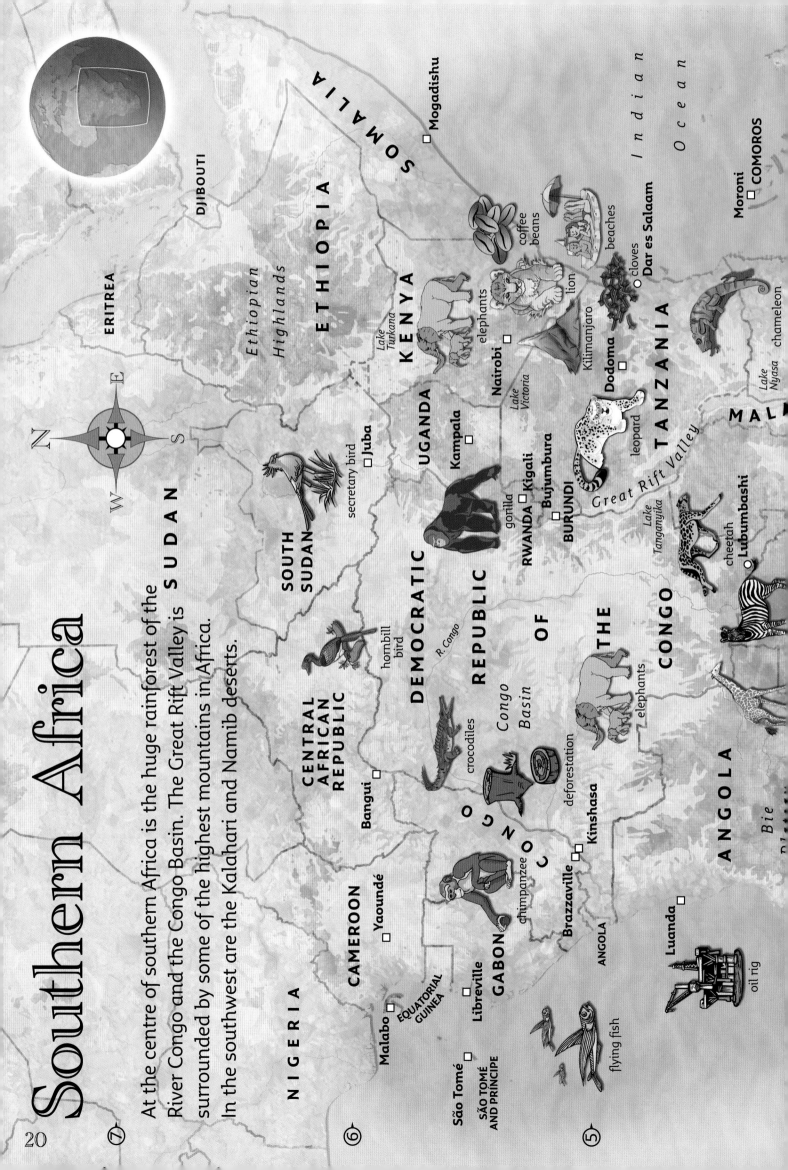

N

W E

S

ERITREA

DJIBOUTI

SOMALIA

Mogadishu

ETHIOPIA

Ethiopian Highlands

SUDAN

Lake Turkana

KENYA

secretary bird

Juba

SOUTH SUDAN

UGANDA

Nairobi

elephants

coffee beans

lion

Kilimanjaro

Dar es Salaam

beaches

cloves

Indian

Ocean

Moroni

COMOROS

Kampala

Lake Victoria

Dodoma

leopard

chameleon

TANZANIA

Lake Nyasa

MAL

Great Rift Valley

Lake Tanganyika

Kigali

RWANDA

Bujumbura

BURUNDI

gorilla

CENTRAL AFRICAN REPUBLIC

hornbill bird

Bangui

DEMOCRATIC

REPUBLIC

OF

THE

CONGO

R. Congo

Congo Basin

elephants

deforestation

cheetah

Lubumbashi

crocodiles

Kinshasa

C O N G O

Brazzaville

ANGOLA

NIGERIA

CAMEROON

Yaoundé

Malabo

EQUATORIAL GUINEA

Libreville

GABON

chimpanzee

São Tomé

SÃO TOMÉ AND PRÍNCIPE

flying fish

Luanda

ANGOLA

Bie

oil rig

⑥

⑤

MADAGASCAR
crocodiles · Antananarivo · lemur

Mozambique Channel

aardvark · port

MOZAMBIQUE

Harare · **ZIMBABWE** · rhinoceros · R. Limpopo
Victoria Falls

Maputo · Mbabane · **SWAZILAND** · Zulu warrior · Zulu house · Durban

NAMIBIA · Windhoek · rugby · rhinoceros · sand dunes · *Namib* Desert · sardines

BOTSWANA · Gaborone · *Kalahari Desert* · meerkat · oryx

Pretoria · Johannesburg · gold mines · Maseru · **LESOTHO** · *Drakensberg* · R. Orange

oranges · grapes · ostrich · **Cape Town** · *Cape of Good Hope* · penguins

REPUBLIC OF SOUTH AFRICA · cricket · **Port Elizabeth**

Atlantic Ocean

sharks

What am I?

- I am found on the coast and in deserts.
- I can be made from worn down stone and shell.
- I move in the wind and get very hot in the sun.
- I can be different shapes: ridges, crescents and crests like waves.
- I can fall downhill in an avalanche, like snow.
- I am made from sand.

What am I?

Try this?

There are lots of different fruits and plants in this region.
Look at the map and find

2 types of fruit
1 type of spice.

Answers at the back of the atlas.

Did you know?

- Madagascar is the only place in the world where lemurs live.
- A lemur is a type of monkey with a long tail.
- Nelson Mandela became the first black president of South Africa in 1994.
- European languages such as French, Portuguese and English are widely spoken in southern Africa.
- Diamonds and gold are mined in southern Africa.

It's a fact

Gorillas are the largest type of ape in the world. They live on the ground in the forests of Africa. Gorillas are a close relative to humans. They eat fruits, leaves and insects. Gorillas are in danger of becoming extinct.

Europe

The land area of Europe covers just over 2% of the world. It is the second smallest continent and extends far north into the Arctic Ocean and south to the Mediterranean Sea. In the north the winters are long and cold. In the south the weather is much warmer. Europe has over 40 countries and a wide variety of cultures, languages and religions.

People facts
- Population: 586 000 000 (excluding Russian Federation)
- Country with most people: Germany 82 689 000
- City with most people: Paris 9 854 000

Geography facts
- Area: 9 908 599 square kilometres (3 825 731 square miles)
- Largest country: Ukraine 603 700 square kilometres (233 090 square miles) (excluding Russian Federation)
- Longest river: Volga 3688 kilometres (2291 miles)
- Highest mountain: El'brus 5642 metres (18 510 feet)
- Largest lake: Caspian Sea 371 000 square kilometres (143 243 square miles)
- Largest island: Great Britain 218 476 square kilometres (84 354 square miles)

Try this!
How many flags are black, red and yellow?

Which flag has 5 blue stripes?

Which country uses this flag?

Answers at the back of the atlas.

ICELAND
□ Reykjavík

Faroe Islands (Denmark)

UNITED KINGDOM

Dublin
□

Great Britain

NETHERLA
Amster
The □
Hague □
Bru
□

London □

BELGIUM

Paris □

LUXEMBO

FRANCE

SWITZER

ANDORRA

MONAC

IRELAND

PORTUGAL

□ **Madrid**

Barcelona

Lisbon □

SPAIN

Gibraltar (UK)

Atlantic Ocean

A F R I C

Ⓐ   Ⓑ   Ⓒ

Arctic Ocean

ASIA

Ural Mountains

Scandinavia

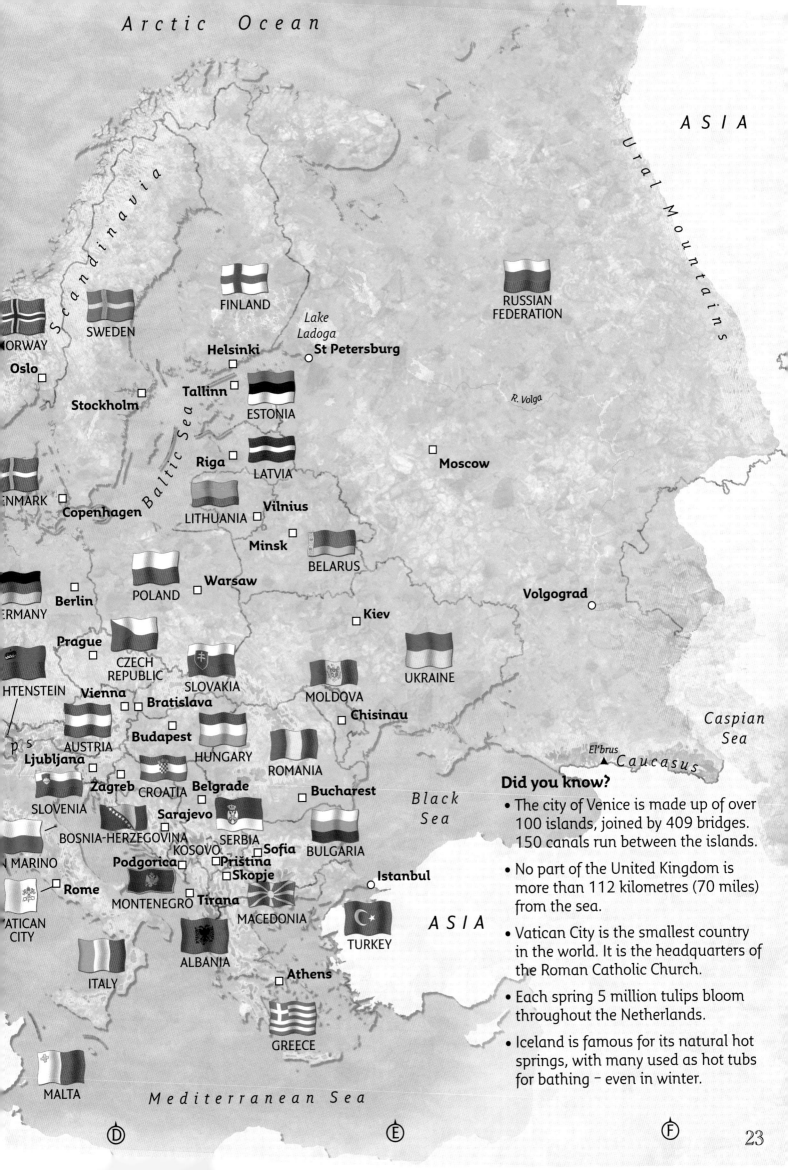

NORWAY

Oslo

SWEDEN

FINLAND

Lake Ladoga

○ St Petersburg

RUSSIAN FEDERATION

Helsinki

R. Volga

Stockholm

Baltic Sea

Tallinn

ESTONIA

Riga

LATVIA

Moscow

DENMARK

Copenhagen

Vilnius

LITHUANIA

Minsk

BELARUS

Volgograd ○

GERMANY

Berlin

POLAND

Warsaw

Kiev

LIECHTENSTEIN

Prague

CZECH REPUBLIC

SLOVAKIA

MOLDOVA

UKRAINE

Vienna

Bratislava

Caspian Sea

Budapest

Chisinau

AUSTRIA

HUNGARY

El'brus

▲ *Caucasus*

Ljubljana

Zagreb

CROATIA

ROMANIA

SLOVENIA

Belgrade

Bucharest

Black Sea

Sarajevo

BOSNIA-HERZEGOVINA

SERBIA

KOSOVO

Sofia

BULGARIA

SAN MARINO

Podgorica

Priština

Rome

Skopje

Istanbul ○

VATICAN CITY

MONTENEGRO

Tirana

MACEDONIA

ASIA

ALBANIA

TURKEY

ITALY

Athens

GREECE

MALTA

Mediterranean Sea

Did you know?

- The city of Venice is made up of over 100 islands, joined by 409 bridges. 150 canals run between the islands.

- No part of the United Kingdom is more than 112 kilometres (70 miles) from the sea.

- Vatican City is the smallest country in the world. It is the headquarters of the Roman Catholic Church.

- Each spring 5 million tulips bloom throughout the Netherlands.

- Iceland is famous for its natural hot springs, with many used as hot tubs for bathing – even in winter.

D   E   F   23

United Kingdom and Ireland

⑦

The United Kingdom is made up of 4 nations: England, Wales, Scotland and Northern Ireland. Its capital and largest city is London. Great Britain is the largest island in Europe and is separated from mainland Europe by only 35 kilometres (21 miles) at the Strait of Dover. Ireland, whose capital is Dublin, is a separate country from Northern Ireland.

⑥

Did you know?

- More than 6000 islands make up the United Kingdom and Ireland.
- Some areas of Ireland have more wet days than dry days.
- The city of Edinburgh is built on an extinct volcano.
- More than 300 different languages are spoken in London.
- The Welsh language is spoken and written in Wales.
- Many tourists come to these islands to visit the castles, churches and ancient buildings.
- Football, rugby and cricket are popular sports.

What am I?

- I am green. Mostly I have white flowers.
- I usually have 3 leaves.
- Ancient people thought I was magical.
- I am strongly associated with Ireland.

What am I?

Answers at the back of the atlas.

Try this!

⑤

Many different sports are popular in the United Kingdom. Look at the map and find
3 sports played with a ball
1 sport that takes place on water
2 sports that need ice or snow

Answers at the back of the atlas.

Shetland Islands

Orkney Islands

Atlantic Ocean

The Minch

Lewis

Skye

Outer Hebrides

Inner Hebrides

golden eagle

Highland cattle

Moray Firth

Inverness

Loch Ness

Ben Nevis

Fort William

Grampian Mts

SCOTLAND

skiing

oil rig

Aberdeen

fishing boat

Highland piper

Dundee

Edinburgh

Firth of Forth

Edinburgh Castle

Glasgow

curling

Jura

Islay

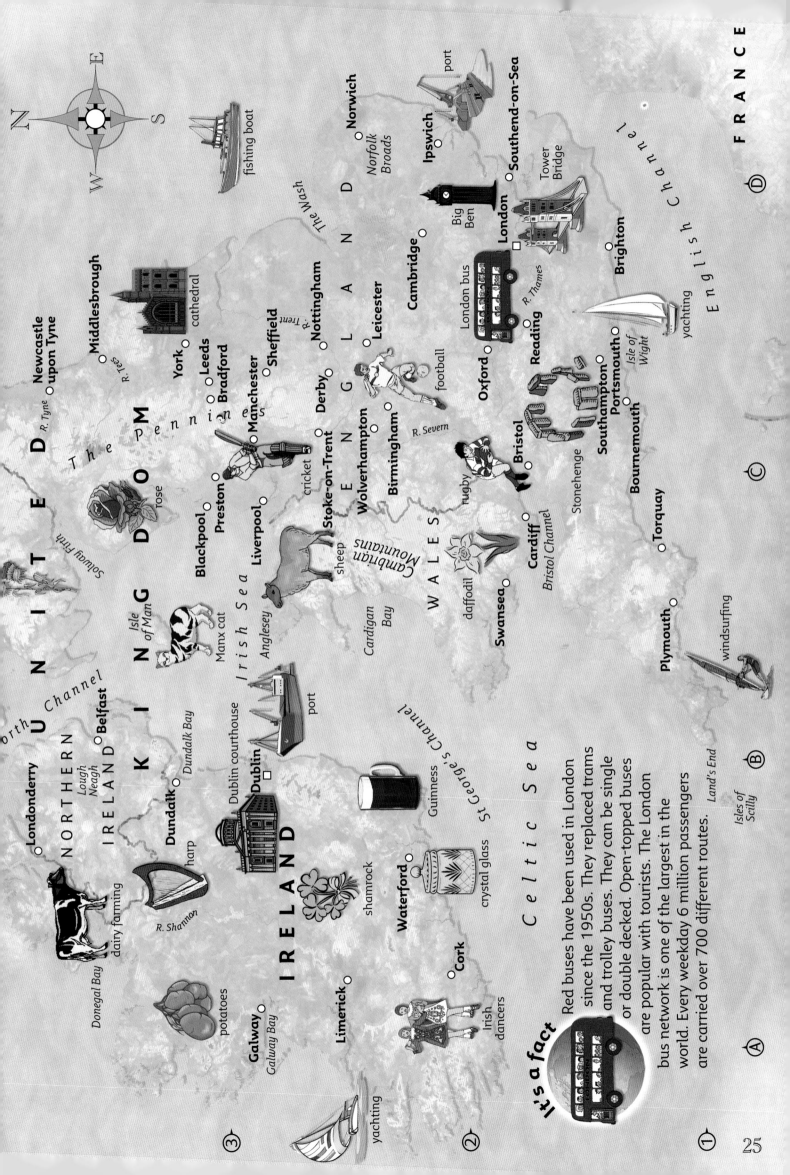

N · E · W · S

fishing boat

FRANCE

English Channel

Norwich

Norfolk Broads

Ipswich

port

Southend-on-Sea

Tower Bridge

Big Ben

London

London bus

R. Thames

Reading

Brighton

yachting

Isle of Wight

The Wash

Cambridge

Leicester

football

Oxford

Portsmouth

Southampton

Bournemouth

Stonehenge

Torquay

Plymouth

windsurfing

Land's End

Isles of Scilly

Celtic Sea

Middlesbrough

cathedral

Newcastle upon Tyne

R. Tees

York

Leeds
Bradford

R. Tyne

The Pennines

rose

Manchester

Sheffield

R. Trent

Nottingham

Derby

cricket

Stoke-on-Trent

U · N · I · T · E · D

Solway Firth

Blackpool
Preston

Liverpool

Irish Sea

K · I · N · G · D · O · M

E · N · G · L · A · N · D

Wolverhampton

Birmingham

R. Severn

rugby

Bristol

Bristol Channel

Cardiff

W · A · L · E · S

Cambrian Mountains

daffodil

Swansea

sheep

Cardigan Bay

Anglesey

Isle of Man

Manx cat

North Channel

Londonderry

N · O · R · T · H · E · R · N

Lough Neagh

Belfast

I · R · E · L · A · N · D

Dundalk Bay

Dundalk

harp

Dublin courthouse

Dublin

port

dairy farming

Donegal Bay

R. Shannon

potatoes

Galway

Galway Bay

Limerick

I · R · E · L · A · N · D

shamrock

Guinness

St George's Channel

Waterford

crystal glass

Cork

Irish dancers

yachting

It's a fact

Red buses have been used in London since the 1950s. They replaced trams and trolley buses. They can be single or double decked. Open-topped buses are popular with tourists. The London bus network is one of the largest in the world. Every weekday 6 million passengers are carried over 700 different routes.

Northern Europe

glaciers
□ **Reykjavík**
ICELAND

Northern Europe has a rugged landscape and many of its countries are almost completely surrounded by sea. In the far north winters can be extremely cold and the seas may freeze for several months. Most people live in the south of this region where the climate is milder.

Faroe Is (Denmark)

Did you know?
- The Baltic Sea borders on 9 countries. Parts of it can be frozen for 6 months of the year.
- Brittany is a region in northwest France. The people there speak Breton.
- Puppets are popular in the Czech Republic. They are used to entertain people and tell stories.
- German is spoken in Austria, Switzerland and Germany.

What am I?
- I have large round eyes, a sharp beak and claws.
- I fly about at night and I sleep during the day.
- I hunt small animals, insects and fish.
- I build nests in trees, barns and sometimes underground.

What am I?

Try this!
Many different types of food are grown or manufactured in this region. Look at the map and find

1 type of cheese
3 types of farm animal
1 type of pastry

Answers at the back of the atlas.

fishing boats

salmon

Highland piper

oil rigs

Norweg churc

DE

shamrock

Edinburgh Castle

North Sea

IRELAND
□ **Dublin**
harp

UNITED

sheep

pig

windmills

KINGDOM
rugby
Tower Bridge
□ **London**

Amsterdam □
The Hague □

NETHERLANDS

Gouda cheese

Atlantic Ocean

English Channel

□ **Brussels**
BELGIUM

R. Rhine

G E

LUXEMBOURG
Luxembourg □

Frankf

Mont St Michel

R. Loire

Paris □
Arc de Triomphe
Eiffel Tower

R. Seine

owl

seafood

Bay of Biscay

F R A N C E

Bern
SWITZERLAN

26

Ⓐ

Ⓑ

croissants

Massif Central

Ⓒ

I T

Arctic Ocean

blue whale

puffin

eider duck

owl

Lappland

Kola Peninsula

fishing through ice

nming

reindeer

wild mushrooms

White Sea

wheat farming

R. Northern Dvina

moose

paper making

lynx

Gulf of Bothnia

FINLAND

Lake Onega

RUSSIAN

skiing

saunas

Lake Ladoga

St Petersburg

beavers

R. Sukhona

wild horses

Oslo

Helsinki

Winter Palace

FEDERATION

Vänern

Stockholm

Tallinn

ESTONIA

dairy cows

Moscow

Vättern

LATVIA

Kremlin

Volga

badger

Riga

R. Dvina

Uplands

K

LITHUANIA

potatoes

openhagen

RUS. FED.

Vilnius

R. Dnieper

wind farms

North European

Minsk

Russian dolls

Elbe

BELARUS

Uplands

Berlin

R. Vistula

boar

Warsaw

It's a fact

POLAND

glass making

brown bears

UKRAINE

Glass is made from sand. The sand is heated to a high temperature until it melts. Many items we use every day are made from glass. It is transparent – we can see through it. Sometimes metals are added to glass to change its colour. Brightly coloured stained glass is often found in church windows.

otball

Prague

CZECH REPUBLIC

R. Dniester

nich

SLOVAKIA

MOLDOVA

castle

Bratislava

Vienna

R. Danube

Budapest

Chisinau

s

AUSTRIA

HUNGARY

castle

ROMANIA

D

E

F

27

Southern Europe

DENMARK

North Sea

⑤

N
W E
S

UNITED KINGDOM

NETHERLANDS
Amsterdam
The Hague
London

Hamburg

Hannover

Berli

R. Rhine

GERMAN

Brussels

Cologne

BELGIUM

Frankfurt

LUXEMBOURG

English Channel

R. Seine

Paris

Eiffel Tower

Swiss cheese

football

Munich

④

Atlantic Ocean

apples

R. Loire

Arc de Triomphe

FRANCE

croissants

grapes

cheese

Bern

LIECHTENSTEIN

SWITZERLAND

AU

gondola

seafood

Bay of Biscay

Massif Central

Mont Blanc

cathedral

Milan

R. Po

Cantabrian Mts

R. Rhône

skiing

A

swordfish

wine

garlic

Apennines

cars

SAN
MA

Oporto

bull fighting

skiing

Marseille

MONACO

Leaning Tower of Pisa

③

Spanish guitar

Pyrenees

ANDORRA

casinos

R. Tagus

Madrid

Barcelona

port

Rome

Va

Lisbon

SPAIN

leather goods

Colosseum

PORTUGAL

beaches

cruise ships

Sardinia

sardines

oranges

flamenco dancers

almonds

Balearic Islands

grapes

Tyrrhenian Sea

Strait of Gibraltar

M
e
d
i
t
e
r

Sic

②

MOROCCO

ALGERIA

TUNISIA

The south of this region lies on the shores of the warm
Mediterranean Sea where many people spend their holidays.
Southern Europe and Africa are separated by only 15 kilometres
(9 miles) of water known as the Strait of Gibraltar, which links the
Atlantic Ocean and the Mediterranean Sea. Two of the world's
smallest countries, Vatican City and Monaco, are in Southern Europe.

①

A
F
R

Ⓐ   Ⓑ   Ⓒ

It's a fact

A gondola is a traditional, long, narrow rowing boat used for transport on the canals in Venice. It is made from 8 different types of wood and is always painted black. Only one oar is used to push a gondola forward in the water.

POLAND

Warsaw

cathedral

Kiev

UKRAINE

gue
ZECH
'UBLIC

glass making

SLOVAKIA

Carpathian Mts

brown bears

R. Dniester

MOLDOVA

Chisinau

na
Bratislava

HUNGARY

Budapest

VENIA
Hungarian
church

bljana

Zagreb

'ATIA

Croatian
house

Belgrade

castle

ROMANIA

Bucharest

Black
Sea

BOSNIA-
HERZEGOVINA

Sarajevo

SERBIA

R. Danube

roses

grapes

Balkan Mts

MONTENEGRO

Priština

Sofia

iatic Sea

Podgorica

KOSOVO

Skopje

BULGARIA

Istanbul

Tirana

ALBANIA

MACEDONIA

pizza
es

pizza

olives

Greek pottery

GREECE

Izmir

TURKEY

fortress

ghetti

Greek
church

Aegean
Sea

Athens

kebabs

Ionian
Sea

Parthenon

lcano

letta
A

Cretan
mosque

Crete

Knossos

fishing boats

n

e

a

n

S

e

a

LIBYA

EGYPT

ICA

C

A

D E F

29

Did you know?

- The islands of Sicily and Sardinia belong to Italy.
- Venice is built on a large area of water, called a lagoon.
- In Albania and Bulgaria nodding your head means no. Shaking your head from side to side means yes.
- In France April Fool's Day is known as April Fish Day.
- Portugal has the world's largest solar powered electricity plant.
- The wristwatch was invented in Switzerland.
- The River Danube flows through 7 countries.

What am I?

- I am made from flour, and egg or water.
- I am cooked quickly in boiling water.
- I am often covered in tomato sauce.
- My name means 'thin string'.
- I am a type of pasta.

What am I?

Answers at the back of the atlas.

Try this!

Many famous buidings and ruins are found in this region.
Look at the map and find

Arc de Triomphe
Colosseum
Knossos
Parthenon
Leaning Tower of Pisa

Asia

⑤

Asia is the largest continent. It is bigger than Europe
and Africa combined. Asia extends from the Ural
mountains to the Pacific Ocean in the east and from
the Arctic Ocean to the Indian Ocean in the south.
Climates vary from the cold Arctic in the north to
hot tropical in the south.

N
W E
S

Arcti

☐ Moscow

E U R O P E

RUSSIAN
FEDERATIO

④

S   i

Ural Mountains

☐ Astana

*Black
Sea*

☐ Ankara

CYPRUS

TURKEY

GEORGIA

T'bilisi

Yerevan

KAZAKHSTAN

LEBANON

☐ Baku   UZBEKISTAN

AZERBAIJAN

Bishkek ☐

ISRAEL

☐ SYRIA   ARMENIA   *Caspian
Sea*

Damascus

Tashkent

KYRGYZSTAN

☐ Amman   Baghdad

TURKMENISTAN

③

JORDAN

☐ Tehran   Ashgabat ☐

Dushanbe ☐

TAJIKISTAN

Kunlun Shan

IRAQ

Kabul ☐

BAHRAIN

Kuwait
KUWAIT   IRAN   AFGHANISTAN

Islamabad ☐

*Plateau
of Tibet*

Himalaya

SAUDI ARABIA

☐ Riyadh

The Gulf

New
Delhi ☐

NEPAL ☐   ☐ BHUTA

QATAR

PAKISTAN

Kathmandu   *Mount
Everest*   Thimph

Red Sea

UNITED ARAB
EMIRATES   ☐ Muscat

Dhaka
☐

②

A F R I C A

☐ San'a

OMAN

INDIA

BANGLADESH

MYAN
(BUR

Naypyid

YEMEN

Try this!

*Socotra
(Yemen)*

*Arabian
Sea*

*Bay of
Bengal*

Yang
(Rang

This country is also an island.
Can you name it?

*Andaman Is
(India)*

SRI LANKA   *Nicobar Is
(India)*

Sri Jayewardenepura Kotte

①

MALDIVES

I n d i a n   O c e a n

Ⓐ   Ⓑ   Ⓒ

Ocean

Bering
Sea

Sea of
Okhotsk

r i a

Lake
Baikal

Ulan Bator

NGOLIA

NORTH KOREA

Sea
of
Japan
(East Sea)

JAPAN

Tokyo

Pyongyang

Beijing

Seoul

CHINA

SOUTH KOREA

East
China
Sea

Pacific

Chang Jiang

Ocean

Taiwan

Hanoi

LAOS

Vientiane

South
China
Sea

Manila

PALAU

Melekeok

angkok

CAMBODIA

PHILIPPINES

Phnom Penh

VIETNAM

HAILAND

BRUNEI

Kuala
umpur

MALAYSIA

Bandar Seri
Begawan

rajaya

Singapore

Borneo

SINGAPORE

INDONESIA

EAST TIMOR

O C E A N I A

Jakarta

Dili

D

E

F

People facts

- Population: 4 085 000 000
  (including Russian Federation)

- Country with most people:
  China 1 323 345 000

- City with most people:
  Tokyo 35 327 000

Geography facts

- Area: 45 036 492 square kilometres
  (17 388 686 square miles)

- Largest country: Russian Federation
  17 075 400 square kilometres
  (6 592 849 square miles)

- Longest river: Chang Jiang
  6380 kilometres (3964 miles)

- Highest mountain: Mount Everest
  8848 metres (29 028 feet)

- Largest lake: Caspian Sea
  371 000 square kilometres
  (143 243 square miles)

- Largest island: Borneo
  745 561 square kilometres
  (287 863 square miles)

Did you know?

- More than half of the world's people
  live in Asia.

- Lake Baikal, in Siberia, is the deepest
  lake in the world.

- The Chinese invented paper, ink, the
  compass and silk.

- Indonesia has more active volcanoes
  than any other country.

- The Dead Sea is so salty bathers can
  float on top of the water.

- The Siberian tiger is the largest living
  cat in the world.

- The red dot in the centre of the
  Japanese flag represents a red sun.

Russian Federation

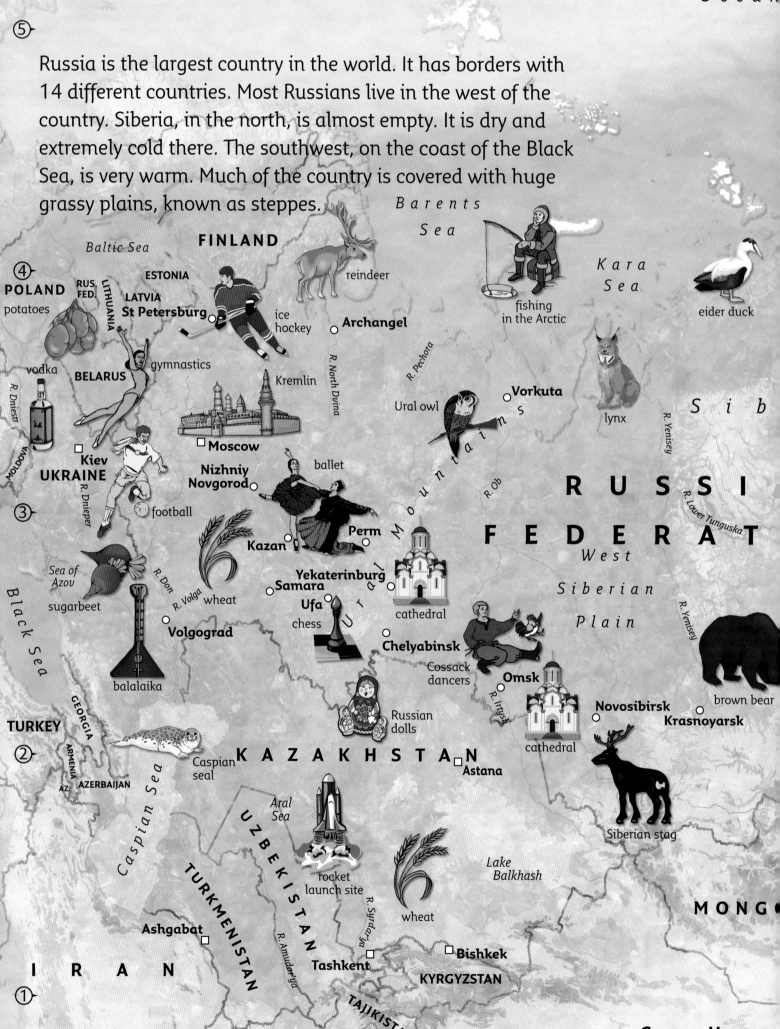

Arctic Ocean

⑤

Russia is the largest country in the world. It has borders with 14 different countries. Most Russians live in the west of the country. Siberia, in the north, is almost empty. It is dry and extremely cold there. The southwest, on the coast of the Black Sea, is very warm. Much of the country is covered with huge grassy plains, known as steppes.

Baltic Sea

FINLAND

Barents Sea

reindeer

fishing in the Arctic

Kara Sea

eider duck

ESTONIA

④
POLAND
potatoes

RUS. FED.

LITHUANIA

LATVIA

St Petersburg

ice hockey

Archangel

R. North Dvina

R. Pechora

Vorkuta

Ural owl

lynx

Si b

vodka

BELARUS

gymnastics

Kremlin

Ural Mountains

R. Ob

R. Yenisey

R U S S I

Kiev
UKRAINE

football

Moscow

Nizhniy Novgorod

ballet

Perm

R. Lower Tunguska

F E D E R A T

③

Kazan

Yekaterinburg

cathedral

West Siberian Plain

R. Yenisey

Sea of Azov

R. Don

R. Volga

wheat

Samara

Ufa

chess

brown bear

sugarbeet

Black Sea

balalaika

Volgograd

Chelyabinsk

Cossack dancers

R. Irtysh

Omsk

cathedral

Novosibirsk

Krasnoyarsk

TURKEY

GEORGIA

ARMENIA

②

AZ. AZERBAIJAN

Caspian seal

Russian dolls

K A Z A K H S T A N

Astana

Siberian stag

Caspian Sea

Aral Sea

UZBEKISTAN

rocket launch site

R. Syrdarya

Lake Balkhash

wheat

M O N G O

TURKMENISTAN

R. Amudarya

Ashgabat

Tashkent

Bishkek

KYRGYZSTAN

I R A N

①

TAJIKISTAN

AFGHANISTAN

C

H

©

Ⓐ

Ⓑ

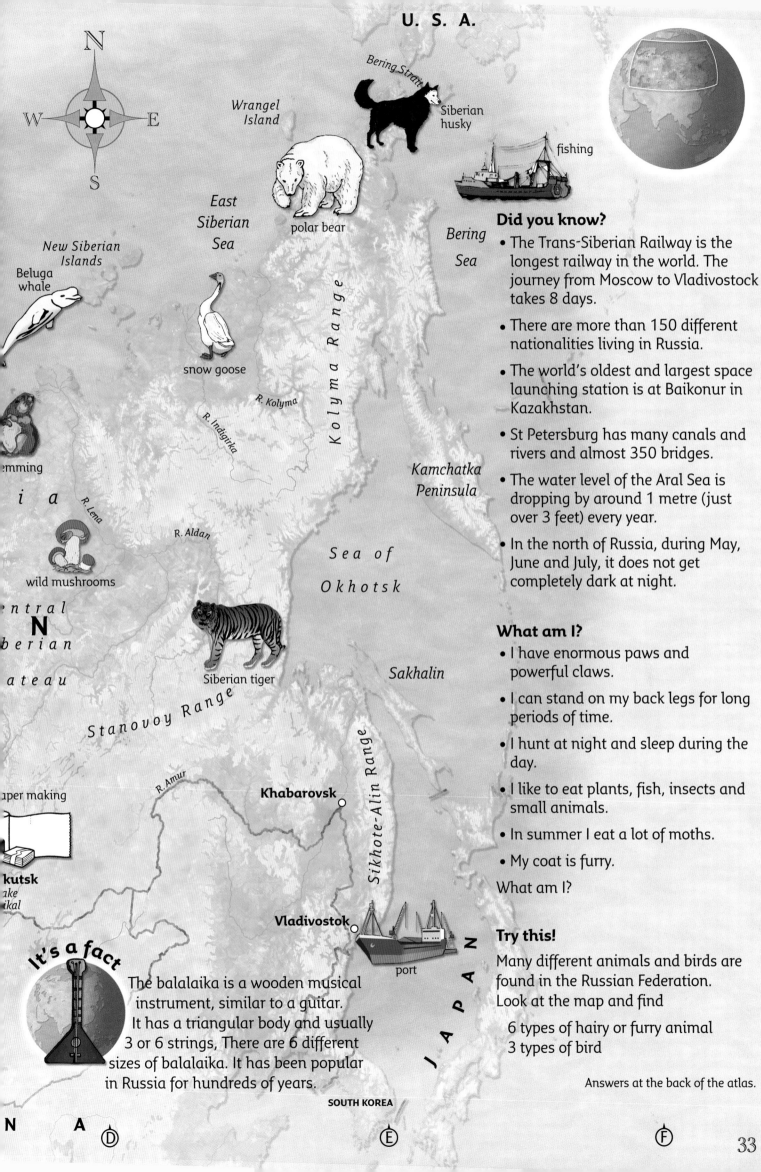

U. S. A.

Bering Strait

Wrangel
Island

Siberian
husky

fishing

New Siberian
Islands

East
Siberian
Sea

Beluga
whale

polar bear

Bering
Sea

snow goose

Kolyma Range

R. Kolyma

R. Indigirka

...mming

...i a

R. Lena

R. Aldan

Kamchatka
Peninsula

wild mushrooms

Sea of

Okhotsk

...ntral

N

...berian

Siberian tiger

Sakhalin

...ateau

Stanovoy Range

Sikhote-Alin Range

R. Amur

Khabarovsk

...per making

...kutsk
...ke
...ikal

Vladivostok

port

J A P A N

Did you know?

- The Trans-Siberian Railway is the longest railway in the world. The journey from Moscow to Vladivostock takes 8 days.

- There are more than 150 different nationalities living in Russia.

- The world's oldest and largest space launching station is at Baikonur in Kazakhstan.

- St Petersburg has many canals and rivers and almost 350 bridges.

- The water level of the Aral Sea is dropping by around 1 metre (just over 3 feet) every year.

- In the north of Russia, during May, June and July, it does not get completely dark at night.

What am I?

- I have enormous paws and powerful claws.

- I can stand on my back legs for long periods of time.

- I hunt at night and sleep during the day.

- I like to eat plants, fish, insects and small animals.

- In summer I eat a lot of moths.

- My coat is furry.

What am I?

Try this!

Many different animals and birds are found in the Russian Federation. Look at the map and find

6 types of hairy or furry animal
3 types of bird

Answers at the back of the atlas.

It's a fact

The balalaika is a wooden musical instrument, similar to a guitar. It has a triangular body and usually 3 or 6 strings, There are 6 different sizes of balalaika. It has been popular in Russia for hundreds of years.

SOUTH KOREA

N

A
D

E

F

33

Southwest Asia

Black Sea

GREECE

The north and west of this area is mountainous, with high ranges extending through Turkey into Iran. The Arabian Peninsula between the Red Sea and The Gulf is mostly dry sandy desert. Water is scarce in much of Southwest Asia. Two major rivers are the Tigris and Euphrates.

El'bru

GEORG

kebabs

□ Ankara

mosque

coffee

ARME
Yere

Taurus Mts

T U R K E Y

Crusader castles

cedar trees

Nicosia □

CYPRUS

Mediterranean Sea

L I B Y A

Beirut
LEBANON □
ISRAEL □ Damascus

SYRIA

date palms

Bagh□

R. Euphra□

Did you know?

- Saudi Arabia is the world's leading exporter of oil.

- Three of the world's major religions started in this area: Judaism, Christianity and Islam.

- Damascus, the capital of Syria, is one of the oldest cities in the world.

- The Caucasus mountain range protects Armenia, Georgia and Azerbaijan from cold north winds.

Cairo
□

Sphinx

R. Nile

Amman
□ □ JORDAN
Jerusalem

Syrian Desert

Dome of the Rock

oil refineries

I R A

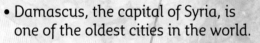
desert safari

Arabian fox *An Nafud*

carpe

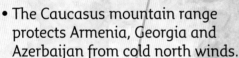
Bedouin tent

What am I?

- I am a type of bird.

- I have long, thin legs and a long neck.

- I like to wade in shallow water.

- I often stand on one leg.

- I eat small shrimps.

- I am pink.

What am I?

E G Y P T

Arabian headdress

Riy□

scuba diving

Najd

crocodile

R. Nile

*R
e
d*

Muslim praying at Mecca

S A U D

angel fish

*A
s
i
r*

Try this!

Look at the map. Can you find these:

3 Arabian animals
1 religious building
1 sport popular in Pakistan

Answers at the back of the atlas.

S U D A N

*S
e
a*

Arabian ho□

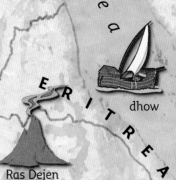
dhow

San'a
□

E
R
I
T
R
E
A

Y E

Ras Dejen

E T H I O P I A

DJIBOUTI

⑤
④
③
②
①

Ⓐ
Ⓑ
Ⓒ

DERATION

Caspian seal

skiing

Caspian Sea

ucasus

bilisi

ZERBAIJAN

Baku

carpets

oil rig

N

Aral Sea

R. Sydar'ya

wheat

space station

KAZAKHSTAN

W   E

S

flamingo

☐ **Tashkent**

UZBEKISTAN

KYRGYZSTAN

CHINA

TURKMENISTAN

R. Amudar'ya

TAJIKISTAN

☐ **Dushanbe**

jackal

Hindu Kush

Karakoram Range

☐ **Ashgabat**

onager

mosque

☐ **Tehran**

Elburz Mts

Zagros Mountains

I R A N

Kabul ☐

AFGHANISTAN

R. Indus

☐ **Islamabad**

Afghan hounds

P A K I S T A N

Sikh

Thar Desert

KUWAIT

☐ **Kuwait**

The Gulf

BAHRAIN

☐ **Manama**

QATAR

☐ **Doha**

oil wells

OMAN

☐ **Abu Dhabi**

UNITED ARAB EMIRATES

Gulf of Oman

R. Indus

Karachi ○

cricket

Mouths of the Indus

I N D I A

RABIA

Arabian camel

oryx

☐ **Muscat**

O M A N

oil tankers

Arabian Sea

ub'al Khali

N

date palms

octopus

date palms

dates

Arabian fishing boats

green turtle

great white shark

Oman

It's a fact

The oryx is a type of antelope. with long, straight horns. The oryx became extinct in the Arabian Peninsula in the 1970s. It has been re-introduced but it is being hunted for its horn. This animal can live in the desert without water for long periods.

D

E

F

35

South Asia

⑦ South Asia is a region of contrasting landscapes and weather. In the north is the great mountain range of Himalaya where the climate is harsh and few people live. The lands at the mouths of the Ganges river are low lying and flooding occurs during the heavy rains in the monsoon season. Most people live in the river valleys, plains and big cities.

N E W S

What am I?

- I live in the sea, especially around coral reefs.
- I have 3 hearts and my blood is blue.
- My soft body means that I can squeeze through small spaces.
- I have a beak.
- I have 8 arms.

What am I?

Try this!

Many different animals, birds and fish are found in this region. Look at the map and find

3 members of the cat family
2 types of bird
1 type of animal with sharp spines

Answers at the back of the atlas.

C H I N A

K u n l u n   S h a n

P l a t e a u   o f   T i b e t

yak

Tibetan monks

□ **Lhasa**

R. Brahmaputra

Thimphu
□
BHUTAN

Mount Everest

N E P A L

H   i   m   a   l   a   y   a

Kathmandu □

Nepalese

Patna

Indian rhinoceros

K2

Kashmir stag

Golden Temple, Amritsar

Delhi □
New Delhi

Taj Mahal

Jaipur ○

snow leopard

TAJIKISTAN

□ **Dushanbe**

H i n d u   K u s h

mountain goat

Kabul □

AFGHANISTAN

Islamabad □

Lahore ○

Faisalabad ○

Sikh

P A K I S T A N

T h a r   D e s e r t

R. Indus

jackal

Afghan hound

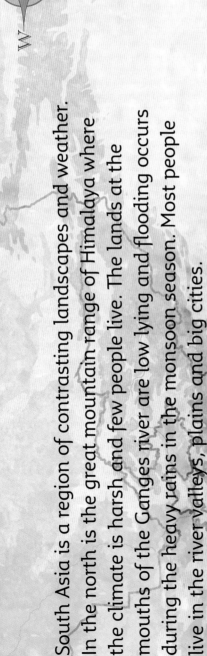

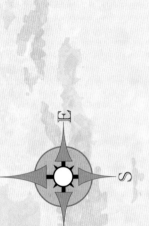

MYANMAR (BURMA)

R. Irrawaddy

Mandalay

Chittagong

INDIA

rice

Kolkata

Mouths of the Ganges

tiger

seafood

Andaman Is (India)

Bay of Bengal

Nicobar Is (India)

parakeet

It's a fact

The sitar is a traditional string instrument with a distinctive sound. It has been popular in India and the surrounding countries for hundreds of years. The body of a sitar is made from a gourd. The neck is made from wood. There can be between 18 and 20 strings. It is a difficult instrument to learn to play.

Indian porcupine

peacock

Eastern Ghats

R. Godavari

Vijayawada

rickshaw

Bhopal

Nagpur

Hyderabad

Chennai

Bangalore

sitar

tea

Sri Jayewardenepura Kotte

Buddhism

SRI LANKA

Indian Ocean

Indore

Deccan

Western Ghats

Trivandrum

MALDIVES

Maldive anemonefish

Ahmadabad

Asiatic lion

hockey

Pune

octopus

coral reefs

Mumbai

port

Arabian Sea

cricket

Did you know?

- The island of Sri Lanka is famous for growing tea.

- There are more than 25 tiger reserves in India, where the animals are protected.

- 8 of the world's 10 highest mountains are in Nepal.

- The Nepalese flag is not rectangular – it is shaped from 2 triangles.

- Many Indian temples own elephants. The animals are decorated and used in religious festivals.

China and Japan

⑤

④

③

②

①

KAZAKHSTAN

Ulan Bator

Mongolian dancers

MONGOLIA

Gobi Desert

Hul.
Nu

Forbid
City

Tien Shan

Bosten Hu

Bactrian camel

Kunlun Shan

K2

snow leopard

Himalaya

Plateau of Tibet

yak

Huang He

Beiji

terracotta soldier

C   H   I   N   A

Pekinese c

Great Wall

Xi'an

bowl of ric

NEPAL

Mount Everest

INDIA

BHUTAN

Chinese vase

Chang Jiang

Wu

chrysanthemum

Chongqing

giant panda

bamboo

firewor

China is a land of high mountains, empty deserts, lush valleys and busy cities. Japan is made up of 4 big islands and over 3500 smaller ones. Lots of people live and work in its big cities. Japan is a hotspot for earthquakes and volcanoes.

gymnastics

Guangzhou

Ho
Ko

VIETNAM

MYANMAR

LAOS

Gulf of Tongking

Hainan

Bay of Bengal

38

Ⓐ

Ⓑ

Ⓒ

RUSSIAN FEDERATION

sperm whale
Sea of Okhotsk

skiing

Sapporo

JAPAN

bonsai tree

Sea of Japan (East Sea)

Harbin

kites

Lake Khanka

Shenyang

NORTH KOREA

karate

Pyongyang

Korea Bay

Buddhist monk
njin

sumo wrestling

Tokyo
Honshu

girl in kimono

Seoul

SOUTH KOREA

electronics industry

bullet train

Yellow Sea

car industry

rice growing

Sakura-jima

puffer fish

rickshaw

Shanghai

East China Sea

chopsticks

Ryukyu Islands

tea

Chinese junk

octopus

pagoda

Taiwan

tuna

port

Pacific Ocean

PHILIPPINES

h *Sea*

Ⓓ   Ⓔ

Did you know?

- Gunpowder was first discovered in China. It can be used to make fireworks and signal flares.

- Chinese is spoken by almost a quarter of all the people in the world.

- China is one of the few countries where fossils of 'Big Foot' (homo gigantus) have been found.

- In Japan the green traffic light is called 'blue'.

- Japan has about 1500 earthquakes each year.

What am I?

- I am made of baked earth.
- My purpose was to protect the first Emperor in the afterlife.
- I was buried in 210-109 BC.
- I was discovered in 1974.
- I belonged to an army.

What am I?

Try this!

China has many different animals. Look at the map and find

The big furry animal who loves to eat bamboo.

Many sports are played in Japan

Can you name 2 of these?

Answers at the back of the atlas.

It's a fact

The giant panda has lived in bamboo forests for several million years. Each year a panda can eat 5 tonnes of bamboo. There are only about 1600 left in the wild.

Southeast Asia

CHINA

Taiwan Strait

Taiwan

⑤ **MYANMAR (BURMA)**

Naypyidaw □

R. Irrawaddy

R. Salween

Hanoi □

Bay of Bengal

Hainan

Buddhist monk

Lu

rubies

temple

satellite launch centre

Vientiane □

Yangon (Rangoon) □

python

Pinatubo – vold

Man

seafood

THAILAND

South China Sea

④

chili peppers

Angkor Wat

R. Mekong

VIETNAM

Bangkok □

Andaman Sea

CAMBODIA

scuba diving

Phnom Penh □

rice growing

Gulf of Thailand

Sul Sea

beaches

oil rig

③

Strait of Malacca

M A L A Y S I A

Kuala Lumpur

BRUNEI □ **Bandar Seri Begawan**

Ce

Putrajaya □

sky scrapers

Sumatra tiger

rubber trees

coral reefs

Singapore **SINGAPORE**

B o r n e o

Macassar Strait

Sumatra

② *Indian Ocean*

rhinoceros

orang utan

water buffa

Java Sea

Cele

temple

Jakarta □

Balinese mask

Southeast Asia is made up of a tropical mainland peninsula, sometimes called Indo-China, and over 20 000 islands. Much of the region is rainforest which has a huge variety of wildlife such as elephants, tigers, orang utans and rhinoceros.

Java

I N D O

Flores

volcano

Komodo dragon

surfing

①

Ⓐ   Ⓑ   Ⓒ

tuna

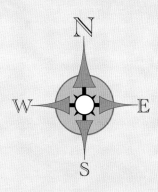

N
W E
S

Pacific

Ocean

it

on

It's a fact

Many rubber tree plantations are found in Southeast Asia. When rubber trees are 5-6 years old they produce latex, collected from slits made in the tree trunk. Latex is made into rubber. The trees produce latex for 20-25 years. They are then cut down and the wood is used to make furniture.

PHILIPPINES

oyster and pearl

Mindanao

pineapples

s

clams

Molucca Sea

coral reefs

coconut
palm tree

E   S   I   A

Banda Sea

Dili
**EAST
TIMOR**

□ **Melekeok**

PALAU

manta
ray

cowrie shell

Puncak Jaya

*New
Guinea*

rubber trees

*A r a f u r a
Sea*

Did you know?

- Singapore is made up of 63 islands.
- The western half of New Guinea is part of Indonesia.
- There are around 150 active volcanoes in Indonesia.
- The Sumatran tiger is the smallest tiger. It is a very fast swimmer.
- A cowrie is the shell of a snail that lives in the sea in tropical areas.

What am I?

- I am a type of lizard.
- I am only found in central Indonesia.
- I have a long body, sharp teeth and strong claws.
- My tongue is long and yellow.
- I am sometimes known as a dragon.

What am I?

Try this!

2 water sports are shown on the map. Can you name them?

Answers at the back of the atlas.

PAPUA NEW

GUINEA

*Coral
Sea*

A   U   S   T   R   A   L   I   A

Ⓓ   Ⓔ   Ⓕ   41

Oceania

⑤

N
W   E
S

FEDERATED STATES
OF MICRONESIA

INDONESIA

▲ Puncak
Jaya

New
Guinea

PAPUA NEW GUINEA

Solomon Sea

□ Port
Moresby

Honia

Arafura Sea

④

Timor Sea

○ Darwin

Gulf
of
Carpentaria

Coral
Sea

Indian
Ocean

Great Barrier Reef

Great
Sandy
Desert

Great Dividing Range

AUSTRALIA

Brisbane ○

③

Great
Victoria
Desert

Lake
Eyre

R. Darling

Great Dividing Range

Perth ○

Great
Australian Bight

R. Murray

Sydney ○

Adelaide ○

□ Canberra

Great

Melbourne ○

Tasman
Sea

Tasmania

②

Hobart ○

Oceania is the smallest continent and lies within the
tropics. It is made up of the countries of Australia, New
Zealand, Papua New Guinea and over 20 000 small Pacific
islands. Australia is by far the largest country and the
majority of the population live on the coast. The central
region of the country is a vast desert known as the outback.
New Zealand is mountainous with a temperate climate and
Papua New Guinea is mainly rainforest.

①

Ⓐ   Ⓑ   Ⓒ

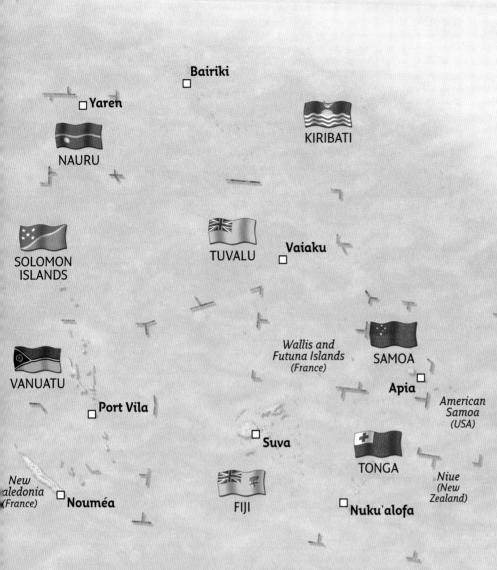

Bairiki
□

□ Yaren

NAURU

KIRIBATI

SOLOMON
ISLANDS

TUVALU

Vaiaku
□

VANUATU

Wallis and
Futuna Islands
(France)

SAMOA

Apia
□

American
Samoa
(USA)

□ Port Vila

□ Suva

TONGA

Niue
(New
Zealand)

New
Caledonia
(France)

Nouméa

FIJI

Nuku'alofa
□

Cook
Islands
(New
Zealand)

FRENCH
POLYNESIA

Did you know?

- 40% of Australia is covered by sand dunes.

- Australia's Great Barrier Reef is the world's largest coral reef.

- In South Island, New Zealand, there are 18 peaks of more than 3000 metres (9842 feet).

- The stars on the flags of Oceanic countries represent the Southern Cross constellation.

- Kangaroos are only found in Australia and New Guinea but there are over 40 different types.

People facts

- Population: 33 000 000

- Country with most people: Australia 20 155 000

- City with most people: Sydney 4 388 000

Geography facts

- Area: 8 844 516 square kilometres (3 414 887 square miles)

- Largest country: Australia 7 692 024 square kilometres (2 969 907 square miles)

- Longest river: Murray-Darling 3750 kilometres (2330 miles)

- Highest mountain: Puncak Jaya 5030 metres (16 502 feet)

- Largest lake: Lake Eyre 0-8900 square kilometres (0-3436 square miles)

- Largest island: New Guinea 808 510 square kilometres (312 167 square miles)

P a c i f i c

O c e a n

○ Auckland

NEW
ZEALAND

*North
Island*

□ Wellington

*South
Island*

Try this!

Which countries do these flags belong to?

Answers at the back of the atlas.

Australia & New Zealand

INDONESIA

The narrow, fertile coast of eastern Australia is separated from the rest of the country by the Great Dividing Range. The highest mountain in Australia, Mount Kosciuszko, is here. New Zealand is made up of two islands. There are volcanoes on North Island. South Island has snowy mountains and glaciers.

rubber trees

New Guinea house

tree kangaroo

PAPUA NEW GUINEA

Solo

Port Moresby

④

Timor Sea

Darwin

boomerang

spiny anteater

Gulf of Carpentaria

Coral Se

Great Barrier Reef

possum

Great Dividing Range

koala

scuba diving

Great Sandy Desert

frilled lizard

dingo

kangaroo

③

wallaby

A U S T R A L I A

Brisb

Uluru (Ayers Rock)

Lake Eyre

Range

Great Victoria Desert

emu

wombat

sheep

R. Darling

parakeet

Sydney Opera House

Sydney

Australian football

Great Australian Bight

Adelaide

cricket

R. Murray

Great Dividing

Canberra

②

Perth

great white shark

black swan

Melbourne

Mount Kosciuszko

surfing

It's a fact

Kiwi fruit are usually the size of a hen's egg. They have hairy brown skin and bright green flesh. The fruit are named after the kiwi bird, the national bird of New Zealand. They are also known as Chinese gooseberries.

Tasmanian devils

Hobart

①

albatross

44

Ⓐ

Ⓑ

Ⓒ

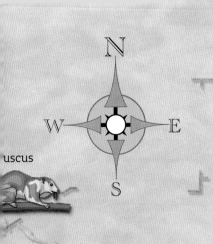

N
W — E
S

uscus

NAURU
□ Yaren

flying fish

KIRIBATI

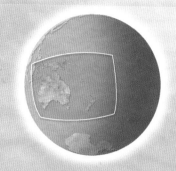

S O L O M O N
I S L A N D S

Honiara □

TUVALU

clown fish

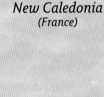

What am I?

- I have powerful back legs, large feet, and use my long tail for balance.
- I like to eat grass and roots.
- I live in groups called mobs.
- As a baby, I live in my mother's pouch.
- I hop around, sometimes very fast.

What am I?

Answers at the back of the atlas.

coconut palms

VANUATU

SAMOA
Apia □

coconuts

FIJI
□ Suva

rugby

bananas

New Caledonia
(France)

□ Port Vila

□ **Nouméa**

Nuku'alofa □ **TONGA**

sea horses

swordfish

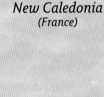
octopus

P a c i f i c   O c e a n

Try this!

There are many kinds of birds and sea creatures in this region. Look at the map and find

1 black bird
4 types of sea creature

Answers at the back of the atlas.

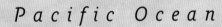
barracudas

kiwi

Auckland ○

rugby

volcanoes

T a s m a n
S e a

kiwi fruit

□ **Wellington**

N E W
Z E A L A N D

sheep

takahe

Did you know?

- This region is on the opposite side of the world to Europe.
- It takes 3 days and 3 nights to cross Australia by train, from Perth to Sydney.
- On South Island, New Zealand, there are more sheep than people.
- There is natural hot steam underground on North Island. The steam is used to produce electricity.
- There are more than 850 native languages used in Papua New Guinea.

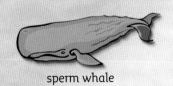
sperm whale

Ⓓ
Ⓔ
Ⓕ
45

The Arctic Ocean

The Arctic Ocean is at the North Pole. Much of the sea is covered in ice all year round. It is the smallest and shallowest ocean in the world.

Try this!

Look at the map and find

1 type of air transport
1 type of water transport
1 type of land transport

Answers at the back of the atlas.

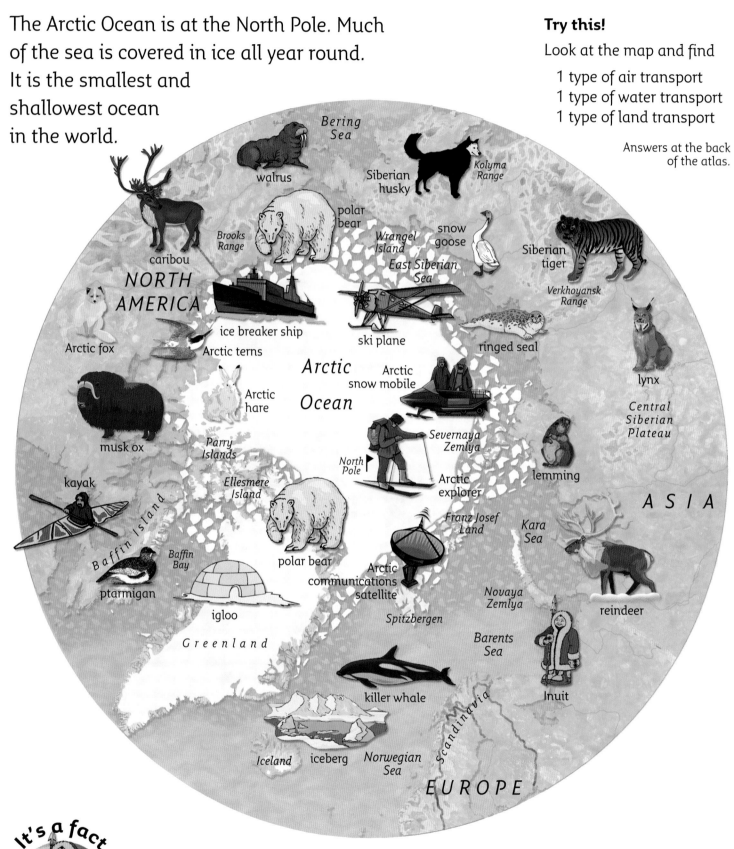

Bering Sea

walrus

Siberian husky

Kolyma Range

polar bear

Brooks Range

Wrangel Island

snow goose

Siberian tiger

East Siberian Sea

Verkhoyansk Range

NORTH AMERICA

ice breaker ship

ski plane

ringed seal

lynx

Arctic fox

Arctic terns

Arctic Ocean

Arctic snow mobile

Central Siberian Plateau

Arctic hare

musk ox

Parry Islands

Severnaya Zemlya

North Pole

Arctic explorer

lemming

ASIA

kayak

Ellesmere Island

polar bear

Franz Josef Land

Kara Sea

Baffin Island

Baffin Bay

Arctic communications satellite

Novaya Zemlya

reindeer

ptarmigan

igloo

Spitzbergen

Greenland

Barents Sea

Inuit

killer whale

Scandinavia

Iceland   iceberg   Norwegian Sea

EUROPE

It's a fact

The Inuit are a group of people native to the coasts of the Arctic Ocean. They have lived there for over 1000 years. Inuit are hunters and fishermen. Mostly they hunt caribou and seal. Inuit fish from boats called kayaks, a type of canoe. They travel across the snow and ice on sledges pulled by teams of dogs. Their language, Inukitut, uses symbols instead of letters.

Did you know?

• The permanent ice of the Arctic Ocean is about 4 metres (13 feet) thick.

• The Arctic is the least salty of all the oceans.

• It never rains in the Arctic Ocean – it only snows.

Antarctica

Antarctica is the area of thick ice surrounding the South Pole. It is the coldest, windiest and driest continent.

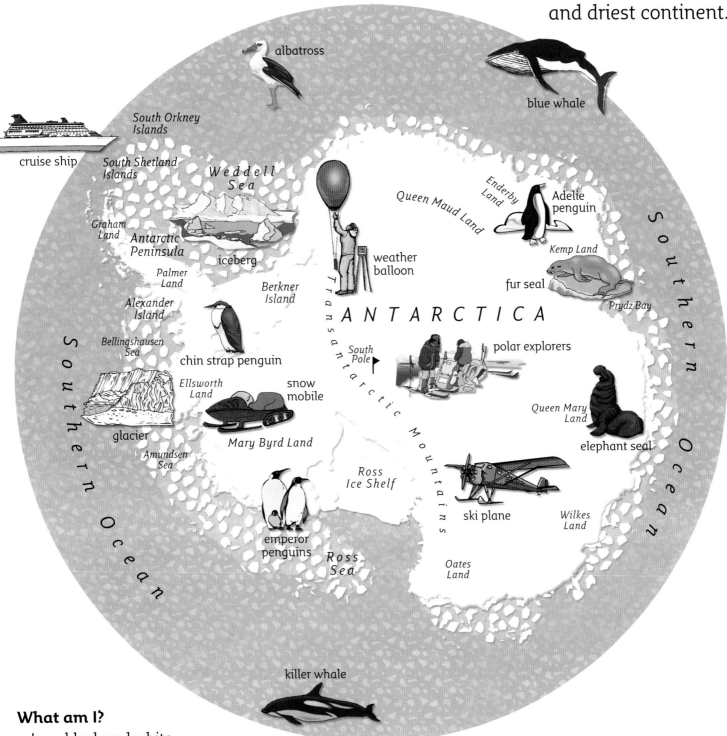

albatross

blue whale

cruise ship

South Orkney Islands

South Shetland Islands

Weddell Sea

Queen Maud Land

Enderby Land

Adelie penguin

Kemp Land

Graham Land

Antarctic Peninsula

iceberg

Palmer Land

Berkner Island

weather balloon

ANTARCTICA

fur seal

Prydz Bay

Alexander Island

Bellingshausen Sea

chin strap penguin

South Pole

polar explorers

Ellsworth Land

snow mobile

Mary Byrd Land

Queen Mary Land

elephant seal

glacier

Amundsen Sea

Ross Ice Shelf

Transantarctic Mountains

ski plane

Wilkes Land

emperor penguins

Ross Sea

Oates Land

Southern Ocean

Southern Ocean

killer whale

What am I?

- I am black and white.
- I eat fish and other sea life.
- I spend half my life on land and half in the sea.
- I am an excellent swimmer.
- On land I waddle on my feet, or slide on my tummy.
- I have wings but cannot fly.

What am I?

Answers at the back of the atlas.

Did you know?

- No one country owns Antarctica.
- No one lives permanently in Antarctica. Scientists visit to learn about the area.
- Many features on Antarctica are named after explorers.

Where have you been?

This world map shows some of the most visited countries in the world. You may have also visited some of these places. Perhaps you spent a holiday or visited friends and relations in these countries.

Look at the comments from children who have spent some time travelling in far away places. Would you agree with their comments or have you more interesting stories to tell?

Barcelona
Barcelona has lots of great shops and the weather is brilliant. It has lots of beaches.
Sophie 10 years

Greece
It's really hot and has lots of outdoor swimming pools and all the times I've been there there's been some really cute cats.
Vicki 10 years

Scotland
I really like the lochs, mountains and forests. The history is definitely the best.
Jake 10 years

Australia
We built sand castles on the beach.
David 6 years

Spain
My favourite place is Salou in Spain because there is a huge theme park, Port Aventura.
Taylor 10 years

London
In London it is very cold in the winter. My Gran lives there. I love London.
Jasmin 10 years

Czech Republic
The Czech Republic is a beautiful place. I visit there with my Gran to see my cousins.
Isaac 10 years

CANADA

UNITED STATES OF AMERICA

BERMUDA

MEXICO

Top 10 countries visited
1. France
2. Spain
3. United States of America
4. China
5. Italy
6. United Kingdom
7. Mexico
8. Germany
9. Turkey
10. Austria

Turkey
The food was nice, especially the lovely cherries from the market near Bodrum! We saw camels and I had a ride on one of them. The best thing was doing back flips on a bungee trampoline.
Charley 10 years

Slovakia
I really liked the snow and building a giant snowman, falling into the snow and skiing.
Marek 4 years

What do you think?

France
I was in France whilst they were in the final of the World Cup. I got to stay up late and make as much noise as I could without being heard.
Calum 10 years

Portugal
I like the swimming pools outside.
Cain 10 years

France
I used to live in France. I will always have this memory. One day it went snowy, sun, snow, sun etc....
Cameron 10 years

GERMANY
UNITED KINGDOM
CZECH REP.
IRELAND
SLOVAKIA
FRANCE
AUSTRIA
ITALY
PORTUGAL
SPAIN
GREECE
TURKEY

CHINA

INDIA

Scotland
The most exciting thing was when I was panning for gold at the Wanlockhead Lead Mine Museum and found some in the bottom of my pan.
Callum 8 years

MALAYSIA

KENYA

AUSTRALIA

SOUTH AFRICA

NEW ZEALAND

Florida
We went to Disneyworld to see Mickey Mouse. It was very hot.
Brad 7 years

Majorca
It is famous because it has a Pirate Show. Its main place is Palma.
Ross 10 years

Scotland
My favourite place is Loch Lomond.
Jordan 10 years

Scotland
I went to Millport. It was thunder and lightning. It struck a lamppost and it fell down on the road.
Antonio 10 years

Scotland
Edinburgh Dungeons has the most scary weirdest monsters in the world. I got the monster stuck in my dreams.
Brian 10 years

Disneyland Paris
Disneyland was great. It was sad when I had to leave.
Daniel 10 years

Spain
I liked Majorca because of the sun and the price of shopping. It was also really good because of the big beaches.
Kieran 10 years

Where have you been?

There are many reasons to travel to far away places. The symbols around this map show a selection of these. Names on the map tell us some of the best places to visit.

More interesting stories are also shown.

Sightseeing

Beach holiday

USA

I like Universal Studio because it has fantastic rides. I would give it a ten out of ten.

Sam 10 years

Winter sports

North America

Rocky Mountains

Kenya

We were in a big car and saw elephants and lions. I liked the lions but they had big teeth. It was very dusty and hot.

Katie 7 years

Caribbean Sea   Cruise

Bird watching

South America

Andes

Desert Sa

USA

I used to live in Vermont. In winter it snows a lot and in the summer it is very hot.

Aidan 10 years

India

India is the greatest place ever.

Naomi 10 years

Malaysia

We went to the jungle and saw lots of animals in the trees. I was scared because the animals made lots of noise at night. It was hot but it rained every day.

Kim 8 years

Exploring

A n

Australia

I love Australia because of all the different animals on land and in the water and all of the lovely weather.

Robbie 10 years

Canary Islands

My favourite place is Tenerife because it's very comfortable...

Darren 10 years

Cadiz, Spain

My feet were almost burnt when I went on the beaches because the sand was so hot. Luckily the water cooled me down.

Helen 10 years

What do you think?

Turkey

It's really HOT!! I sleep walked into the hallway of our dormitory and I had nightmares about one of my Aunt's friend's cousins.

Sean 10 years

Scotland

Arran is an island off the southwest coast of Scotland. The funniest thing is when my friend catapults people across the bedroom with his feet. The best thing was when I got to ride a horse through a river on a pony trek.

Rona 10 years

South Africa

It was hot. We went on a boat and saw fish in the sea. I had a sore tummy in the boat.

Cameron 5 years

Asia

Himalaya

an Sea

a

Africa

East
Africa

Trekking

Greece

Rhodes in Greece is quiet with fantastic beaches.

Martha 10 years

Australia

Wildlife watching

Water sports

Spain

My favourite city is Barcelona because it is very lively.

Megan 10 years

New Zealand

We made snowballs to throw at each other. But it was very cold.

Sophie 8 years

t i c a

Canada

I love Canada because of the cool stuff to see and it is only 1 hour away from Disneyland.

Makeila 10 years

USA

Florida is where I always go with my family. There are lots of things to do like rides and stuff.

Megan 10 years

Ireland

My Great Granny lives in Ireland. It has great restaurants.

Molly 10 years

Bermuda

Bermuda is always peaceful and quiet.

Callum 10 years

Barcelona

Barcelona has lots of great shops and the weather is brilliant. It has lots of beaches.

Sophie 10 years

Countries of the World

Flag	COUNTRY, CONTINENT / Capital City / Population	Area square kilometres (square miles)

AFGHANISTAN, ASIA
Kabul
29 863 000
652 225 (251 825)

ALBANIA, EUROPE
Tirana
3 130 000
28 748 (11 100)

ALGERIA, AFRICA
Algiers
32 854 000
2 381 741 (919 595)

ANGOLA, AFRICA
Luanda
15 941 000
1 246 700 (481 353)

ARGENTINA, SOUTH AMERICA
Buenos Aires
38 747 000
2 766 889 (1 068 302)

ARMENIA, ASIA
Yerevan
3 016 000
29 800 (11 506)

AUSTRALIA, OCEANIA
Canberra
20 155 000
7 692 024 (2 969 907)

AUSTRIA, EUROPE
Vienna
8 189 000
83 855 (32 377)

BAHRAIN, ASIA
Manama
727 000
691 (267)

BANGLADESH, ASIA
Dhaka
141 822 000
143 998 (55 598)

BELARUS, EUROPE
Minsk
9 755 000
207 600 (80 155)

BELGIUM, EUROPE
Brussels
10 419 000
30 520 (11 784)

BENIN, AFRICA
Porto Novo
8 439 000
112 620 (43 483)

BHUTAN, ASIA
Thimphu
2 163 000
46 620 (18 000)

BOLIVIA, SOUTH AMERICA
La Paz/Sucre
9 182 000
1 098 581 (424 164)

BOSNIA-HERZEGOVINA, EUROPE
Sarajevo
3 907 000
51 130 (19 741)

BOTSWANA, AFRICA
Gaborone
1 765 000
581 370 (224 468)

BRAZIL, SOUTH AMERICA
Brasília
186 405 000
8 514 879 (3 287 613)

BRUNEI, ASIA
Bandar Seri Begawan
374 000
5 765 (2 226)

BULGARIA, EUROPE
Sofia
7 726 000
110 994 (42 855)

BURKINA, AFRICA
Ouagadougou
13 228 000
274 200 (105 869)

BURUNDI, AFRICA
Bujumbura
7 548 000
27 835 (10 747)

CAMBODIA, ASIA
Phnom Penh
14 071 000
181 035 (69 884)

CAMEROON, AFRICA
Yaoundé
16 322 000
475 442 (183 569)

CANADA, NORTH AMERICA
Ottawa
32 268 000
9 984 670 (3 855 103)

CENTRAL AFRICAN REPUBLIC, AFRICA
Bangui
4 038 000
622 436 (240 324)

CHAD, AFRICA
Ndjamena
9 749 000
1 284 000 (495 755)

CHILE, SOUTH AMERICA
Santiago
16 295 000
756 945 (292 258)

CHINA, ASIA
Beijing
1 323 345 000
9 620 671 (3 714 562)

COLOMBIA, SOUTH AMERICA
Bogotá
45 600 000
1 141 748 (440 831)

CONGO, AFRICA
Brazzaville
3 999 000
342 000 (132 047)

CONGO, DEMOCRATIC REPUBLIC OF THE AFRICA
Kinshasa
57 549 000
2 345 410 (905 568)

COSTA RICA, NORTH AMERICA
San José
4 327 000
51 100 (19 730)

CÔTE D'IVOIRE, AFRICA
Yamoussoukro
18 154 000
322 463 (124 504)

CROATIA, EUROPE
Zagreb
4 551 000
56 538 (21 829)

CUBA, NORTH AMERICA
Havana
11 269 000
110 860 (42 803)

CYPRUS, ASIA
Nicosia
835 000
9 251 (3 572)

CZECH REPUBLIC, EUROPE
Prague
10 220 000
78 864 (30 450)

DENMARK, EUROPE
Copenhagen
5 431 000
43 075 (16 631)

DJIBOUTI, AFRICA		
Djibouti		23 200
793 000		(8 958)
DOMINICAN REPUBLIC, NORTH AMERICA		
Santo Domingo		48 442
8 895 000		(18 704)
EAST TIMOR, ASIA		
Dili		14 874
947 000		(5 743)
ECUADOR, SOUTH AMERICA		
Quito		272 045
13 228 000		(105 037)
EGYPT, AFRICA		
Cairo		1 000 250
74 033 000		(386 199)
EL SALVADOR, NORTH AMERICA		
San Salvador		21 041
6 881 000		(8 124)
EQUATORIAL GUINEA, AFRICA		
Malabo		28 051
504 000		(10 831)
ERITREA, AFRICA		
Asmara		117 400
4 401 000		(45 328)
ESTONIA, EUROPE		
Tallinn		45 200
1 330 000		(17 452)
ETHIOPIA, AFRICA		
Addis Ababa		1 133 880
77 431 000		(437 794)
FINLAND, EUROPE		
Helsinki		338 145
5 249 000		(130 559)
FRANCE, EUROPE		
Paris		543 965
60 496 000		(210 026)
GABON, AFRICA		
Libreville		267 667
1 384 000		(103 347)
GEORGIA, ASIA		
T'bilisi		69 700
4 474 000		(26 911)
GERMANY, EUROPE		
Berlin		357 022
82 689 000		(137 849)
GHANA, AFRICA		
Accra		238 537
22 113 000		(92 100)
GREECE, EUROPE		
Athens		131 957
11 120 000		(50 949)
GUATEMALA, NORTH AMERICA		
Guatemala City		108 890
12 599 000		(42 043)
GUINEA, AFRICA		
Conakry		245 857
6 402 000		(94 926)
GUINEA-BISSAU, AFRICA		
Bissau		36 125
1 586 000		(13 948)
GUYANA, SOUTH AMERICA		
Georgetown		214 969
751 000		(83 000)
HAITI, NORTH AMERICA		
Port-au-Prince		27 750
8 528 000		(10 714)
HONDURAS, NORTH AMERICA		
Tegucigalpa		112 088
7 205 000		(43 277)
HUNGARY, EUROPE		
Budapest		93 030
10 098 000		(35 919)
ICELAND, EUROPE		
Reykjavik		102 820
295 000		(39 699)
INDIA, ASIA		
New Delhi		3 064 898
1 103 371 000		(1 183 364)
INDONESIA, ASIA		
Jakarta		1 919 445
222 781 000		(741 102)
IRAN, ASIA		
Tehran		1 648 000
69 515 000		(636 296)
IRAQ, ASIA		
Baghdad		438 317
28 807 000		(169 235)
IRELAND EUROPE		
Dublin		70 282
4 148 000		(27 136)
ISRAEL, ASIA		
Jerusalem		20 770
6 725 000		(8 019)
ITALY, EUROPE		
Rome		301 245
58 093 000		(116 311)
JAMAICA, NORTH AMERICA		
Kingston		10 991
2 651 000		(4 244)
JAPAN, ASIA		
Tokyo		377 727
128 085 000		(145 841)
JORDAN, ASIA		
Amman		89 206
5 703 000		(34 443)
KAZAKHSTAN, ASIA		
Astana		2 717 300
14 825 000		(1 049 155)
KENYA, AFRICA		
Nairobi		582 646
34 256 000		(224 961)
KUWAIT, ASIA		
Kuwait		17 818
2 687 000		(6 880)
KYRGYZSTAN, ASIA		
Bishkek		198 500
5 264 000		(76 641)
LAOS, ASIA		
Vientiane		236 800
5 924 000		(91 429)

53

Countries of the World

LATVIA, EUROPE — Riga — 2 307 000	63 700 (24 595)	**NEPAL**, ASIA — Kathmandu — 27 133 000	147 181 (56 827)
LEBANON, ASIA — Beirut — 3 577 000	10 452 (4 036)	**NETHERLANDS**, EUROPE — Amsterdam/The Hague — 16 299 000	41 526 (16 033)
LESOTHO, AFRICA — Maseru — 1 795 000	30 355 (11 720)	**NEW ZEALAND**, OCEANIA — Wellington — 4 028 000	270 534 (104 454)
LIBERIA, AFRICA — Monrovia — 3 283 000	111 369 (43 000)	**NICARAGUA**, NORTH AMERICA — Managua — 5 487 000	130 000 (50 193)
LIBYA, AFRICA — Tripoli — 5 853 000	1 759 540 (679 362)	**NIGER**, AFRICA — Niamey — 13 957 000	1 267 000 (489 191)
LITHUANIA, EUROPE — Vilnius — 3 431 000	65 200 (25 174)	**NIGERIA**, AFRICA — Abuja — 131 530 000	923 768 (356 669)
LUXEMBOURG, EUROPE — Luxembourg — 465 000	2 586 (998)	**NORTH KOREA**, ASIA — Pyongyang — 22 488 000	120 538 (46 540)
MACEDONIA, EUROPE — Skopje — 2 034 000	25 713 (9 928)	**NORWAY**, EUROPE — Oslo — 4 620 000	323 878 (125 050)
MADAGASCAR, AFRICA — Antananarivo — 18 606 000	587 041 (226 658)	**OMAN**, ASIA — Muscat — 2 567 000	309 500 (119 499)
MALAWI, AFRICA — Lilongwe — 12 884 000	118 484 (45 747)	**PAKISTAN**, ASIA — Islamabad — 157 935 000	803 940 (310 403)
MALAYSIA, ASIA — Kuala Lumpur/Putrajaya — 25 347 000	332 965 (128 559)	**PANAMA**, NORTH AMERICA — Panama City — 3 232 000	77 082 (29 762)
MALI, AFRICA — Bamako — 13 518 000	1 240 140 (478 821)	**PAPUA NEW GUINEA**, OCEANIA — Port Moresby — 5 887 000	462 840 (178 704)
MAURITANIA, AFRICA — Nouakchott — 3 069 000	1 030 700 (397 955)	**PARAGUAY**, SOUTH AMERICA — Asunción — 6 158 000	406 752 (157 048)
MEXICO, NORTH AMERICA — Mexico City — 107 029 000	1 972 545 (761 604)	**PERU**, SOUTH AMERICA — Lima — 27 968 000	1 285 216 (496 225)
MONGOLIA, ASIA — Ulan Bator — 2 646 000	1 565 000 (604 250)	**PHILIPPINES**, ASIA — Manila — 83 054 000	300 000 (115 831)
MONTENEGRO, EUROPE — Podgorica — 620 000	13 812 (5333)	**POLAND**, EUROPE — Warsaw — 38 530 000	312 683 (120 728)
MOROCCO, AFRICA — Rabat — 31 478 000	446 550 (172 414)	**PORTUGAL**, EUROPE — Lisbon — 10 495 000	88 940 (34 340)
MOZAMBIQUE, AFRICA — Maputo — 19 792 000	799 380 (308 642)	**QATAR**, ASIA — Doha — 813 000	11 437 (4 416)
MYANMAR (BURMA), ASIA — Naypyidaw/Yangon — 50 519 000	676 577 (261 228)	**ROMANIA**, EUROPE — Bucharest — 21 711 000	237 500 (91 699)
NAMIBIA, AFRICA — Windhoek — 2 031 000	824 292 (318 261)	**RUSSIAN FEDERATION**, EUROPE/ASIA — Moscow — 143 202 000	17 075 400 (6 592 849)

SAUDI ARABIA, ASIA	Riyadh	2 200 000	
	24 573 000	(849 425)	
SENEGAL, AFRICA	Dakar	196 720	
	11 658 000	(75 954)	
SERBIA, EUROPE	Belgrade	88 361	
	9 379 000	(34 116)	
SIERRA LEONE, AFRICA	Freetown	71 740	
	5 525 000	(27 699)	
SINGAPORE, ASIA	Singapore	639	
	4 326 000	(247)	
SLOVAKIA, EUROPE	Bratislava	49 035	
	5 401 000	(18 933)	
SLOVENIA, EUROPE	Ljubljana	20 251	
	1 967 000	(7 819)	
SOMALIA, AFRICA	Mogadishu	637 657	
	8 228 000	(246 201)	
SOUTH AFRICA, REPUBLIC OF AFRICA	Pretoria/Cape Town	1 219 090	
	47 432 000	(470 693)	
SOUTH KOREA, ASIA	Seoul	99 274	
	47 817 000	(38 330)	
SOUTH SUDAN, AFRICA	Juba	644 329	
	8 260 490	(248 777)	
SPAIN, EUROPE	Madrid	504 782	
	43 064 000	(194 897)	
SRI LANKA, ASIA	Sri Jayewardenepura Kotte	65 610	
	20 743 000	(25 332)	
SUDAN, AFRICA	Khartoum	1 861 484	
	36 233 000	(718 723)	
SURINAME, SOUTH AMERICA	Paramaribo	163 820	
	449 000	(63 251)	
SWAZILAND, AFRICA	Mbabane	17 364	
	1 032 000	(6 704)	
SWEDEN, EUROPE	Stockholm	449 964	
	9 041 000	(173 732)	
SWITZERLAND, EUROPE	Bern	41 293	
	7 252 000	(15 943)	
SYRIA, ASIA	Damascus	185 180	
	19 043 000	(71 498)	
TAJIKISTAN, ASIA	Dushanbe	143 100	
	6 507 000	(55 251)	

TANZANIA, AFRICA	Dodoma	945 087	
	38 329 000	(364 900)	
THAILAND, ASIA	Bangkok	513 115	
	64 233 000	(198 115)	
THE GAMBIA, AFRICA	Banjul	11 295	
	1 517 000	(4 361)	
TOGO, AFRICA	Lomé	56 785	
	6 145 000	(21 925)	
TRINIDAD AND TOBAGO, NORTH AMERICA	Port of Spain	5 130	
	1 305 000	(1 981)	
TUNISIA, AFRICA	Tunis	164 150	
	10 102 000	(63 379)	
TURKEY, ASIA/EUROPE	Ankara	779 452	
	73 193 000	(300 948)	
TURKMENISTAN, ASIA	Ashgabat	488 100	
	4 833 000	(188 456)	
UGANDA, AFRICA	Kampala	241 038	
	28 816 000	(93 065)	
UKRAINE, EUROPE	Kiev	603 700	
	46 481 000	(233 090)	
UNITED ARAB EMIRATES, ASIA	Abu Dhabi	77 700	
	4 496 000	(30 000)	
UNITED KINGDOM, EUROPE	London	243 609	
	59 668 000	(94 058)	
UNITED STATES OF AMERICA, NORTH AMERICA	Washington	9 826 635	
	298 213 000	(3 794 085)	
URUGUAY, SOUTH AMERICA	Montevideo	176 215	
	3 463 000	(68 037)	
UZBEKISTAN, ASIA	Tashkent	447 400	
	26 593 000	(172 742)	
VENEZUELA, SOUTH AMERICA	Caracas	912 050	
	26 749 000	(352 144)	
VIETNAM, ASIA	Hanoi	329 565	
	84 238 000	(127 246)	
YEMEN, ASIA	San'a	527 968	
	20 975 000	(203 850)	
ZAMBIA, AFRICA	Lusaka	752 614	
	11 668 000	(290 586)	
ZIMBABWE, AFRICA	Harare	390 759	
	13 010 000	(150 873)	

55

Games and Quizzes

Name the continents

Match the numbers on the map to the continent names listed.

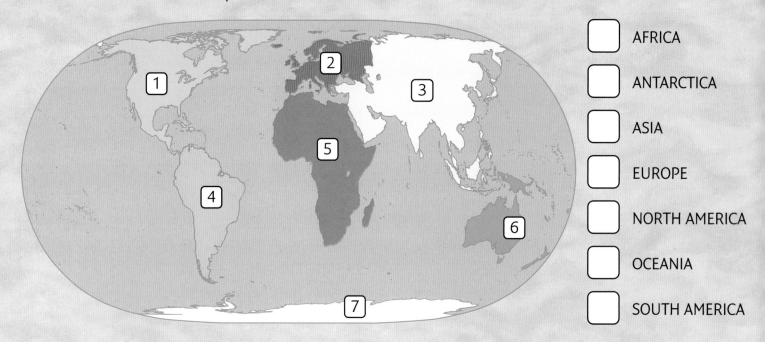

☐ AFRICA

☐ ANTARCTICA

☐ ASIA

☐ EUROPE

☐ NORTH AMERICA

☐ OCEANIA

☐ SOUTH AMERICA

Name the countries

Match the shapes to the country names listed.

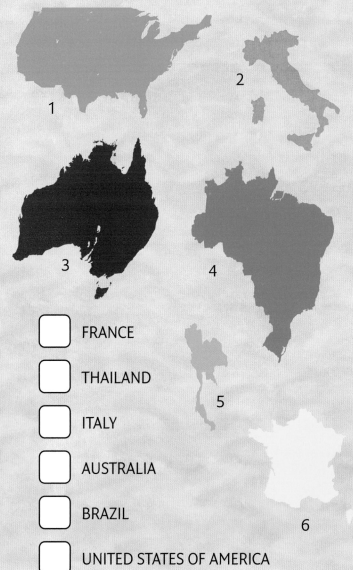

☐ FRANCE

☐ THAILAND

☐ ITALY

☐ AUSTRALIA

☐ BRAZIL

☐ UNITED STATES OF AMERICA

Search for cities

The 12 capital cities listed below are hidden in this grid. See how many you can find.

A	O	W	E	L	L	I	N	G	T	O	N
B	P	X	Z	P	O	J	X	Z	Q	J	O
W	A	S	H	I	N	G	T	O	N	V	T
X	R	K	Y	Y	D	W	V	J	F	X	T
C	I	K	P	F	O	X	Z	Q	J	F	A
A	S	Z	B	A	N	G	K	O	K	X	W
N	J	V	Q	Z	X	X	C	H	Z	Y	A
B	R	A	S	I	L	I	A	W	X	T	V
E	W	H	G	M	X	Z	I	Z	F	U	X
R	O	M	E	X	Q	V	R	J	Q	N	F
R	V	W	T	O	K	Y	O	V	W	I	Q
A	Q	W	H	G	M	X	T	J	V	S	Q

LONDON   WELLINGTON   CAIRO
PARIS   TOKYO   TUNIS
ROME   BANGKOK   OTTAWA
CANBERRA   BRASILIA   WASHINGTON

Quiz 1

1. What is the largest country in the world?

2. What is the capital of France?

3. How many stars are on the flag of China?

Colour match

All these symbols have a colour in part of their name. Find their correct name by matching a colour with one of the other words.

1. _ _ _ _ _ _ _   _ _ _ _ _ _

2. _ _ _ _   _ _ _ _ _ _ _ _

3. _ _ _ _ _   _ _ _ _

4. _ _ _ _ _ _ _ _ _ _

5. _ _ _ _ _   _ _ _ _ _   _ _ _ _ _

blue	flamingo
brown	berries
pink	shark
purple	bear
great white	finch

Unscramble the countries

Rearrange the letters in the boxes to find the names of 6 countries.

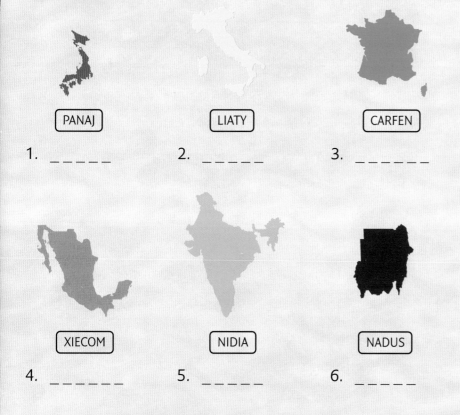

PANAJ

1. _ _ _ _ _

LIATY

2. _ _ _ _ _

CARFEN

3. _ _ _ _ _ _

XIECOM

4. _ _ _ _ _ _

NIDIA

5. _ _ _ _ _

NADUS

6. _ _ _ _ _

Quiz 2

1. What is the world's longest river?

2. How many colours are on the flag of Italy?

3. What kind of bears are found in Arctic regions?

Whose flag is this?

There are 16 country flags and 16 country names shown below. Try to match up the country names to their flag. Add the correct flag number to the box beside each country name.

1. 2.
3. 4.
5. 6.
7. 8.
9. 10.
11. 12.
13. 14.
15. 16.

☐ CHINA	☐ JAPAN
☐ CANADA	☐ GREECE
☐ PAKISTAN	☐ NEPAL
☐ BRAZIL	☐ SOMALIA
☐ CHILE	☐ SWEDEN
☐ AUSTRALIA	☐ KENYA

☐ NEW ZEALAND

☐ UNITED KINGDOM

☐ REPUBLIC OF SOUTH AFRICA

☐ UNITED STATES OF AMERICA

Answers on page 64.

Games and Quizzes

Name the oceans

Match the numbers on the map to the ocean names listed.

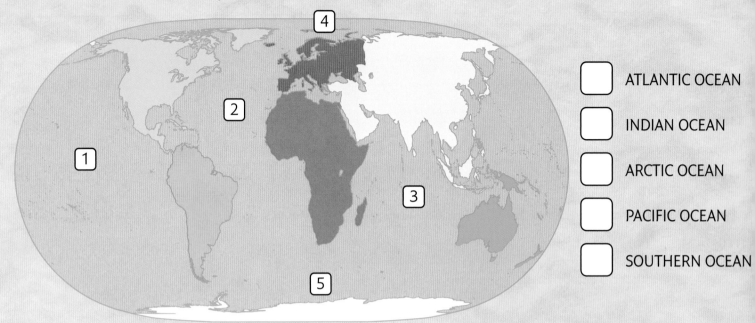

☐ ATLANTIC OCEAN

☐ INDIAN OCEAN

☐ ARCTIC OCEAN

☐ PACIFIC OCEAN

☐ SOUTHERN OCEAN

Name the symbol

Choose a suitable caption for each symbol from the names in the panel on the right.
Only one caption will match each symbol.

Puffin	Kiwi fruit	Owl
	Bobcat	Polar bear
Grapes	Taj Mahal	
Stonehenge	Hockey	Apple
	Banana	Cricket
Walrus	Shamrock	
Oil platform	Sydney Opera House	

1. _____   2. _____

3. _____   4. _____

5. _____   6. _____

Quiz 3

1. What is the capital of Argentina?

2. How many blue stripes appear on the flag of Honduras?

3. In which country would you watch this sport?

Symbol Match

In which country would you expect to see these?
Add the correct symbol number to the box beside each country name.

1. Tower Bridge

2. Croissants

3. Liberty Bell

4. Taj Mahal

5. Kangaroo

6. Zulu house

☐ UNITED STATES OF AMERICA   ☐ FRANCE

☐ UNITED KINGDOM   ☐ SWAZILAND

☐ INDIA   ☐ AUSTRALIA

Which continent are you in?

Look at the groups of flags below.
Which continent would you be in if these flags were shown?

1.

2.

3.

4.

5.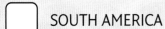

6.

☐ ASIA   ☐ OCEANIA

☐ EUROPE   ☐ NORTH AMERICA

☐ SOUTH AMERICA   ☐ AFRICA

Search for countries

The 10 countries listed below
are hidden in this grid.
See how many you can find.

A	R	G	E	N	T	I	N	A	F	K	Y
N	V	G	F	Y	N	E	Z	U	Z	B	V
C	Y	D	Q	C	G	G	G	S	X	Q	J
H	U	N	G	A	R	Y	B	T	G	B	J
I	L	A	F	N	G	P	H	R	B	O	Q
N	N	L	Z	A	S	T	V	A	P	T	X
A	G	O	X	D	T	V	F	L	H	S	F
H	P	O	L	A	N	D	Z	I	H	W	F
H	Y	X	Q	Q	V	Z	X	A	Z	A	O
M	E	X	I	C	O	G	G	V	G	N	Q
Q	Z	J	B	Y	F	F	B	X	B	A	J
N	I	G	E	R	I	A	B	J	Q	K	P

ARGENTINA

AUSTRALIA

BOTSWANA

CANADA

CHINA

EGYPT

HUNGARY

MEXICO

NIGERIA

POLAND

Quiz 4

1. What is the world's highest mountain?

2. What is the capital of China?

3. In which country would you find these animals?

Answers on page 64.

Index

This index lists all the important place names shown on the maps. The grid code numbers and letters help you to find the correct position of the name on each map.

Answers

	Try this!		**What am I?**
2-3	GREENLAND		
4-5	1. Canadian goose, Arctic tern, snowy owl, snow goose, ptarmigan 2. Newfoundland, husky 3. polar bear, musk ox, Arctic fox, wolf, brown bear, bobcat, caribou, moose, beaver, Arctic hare		A maple leaf
6-7	1. blueberries, grapes, oranges, apples 2. hotdog, hamburger, muffin 3. peanut		A hot dog
8-9	1. tropical fish, sea horse, great white shark, elephant seal, monk seal, turtle 2. parrot, toucan		A cactus
10-11	1. Colombia, Chile	2. Bogota, Brasilia	
12-13	1. emerald, diamond	2. anaconda	A condor
14-15	1. mackerel, sardine 2. polo, skiing, football, motor racing		A killer whale
16-17	MADAGASCAR		
18-19	1. camel, gerbil, baboon 2. scorpion, tortoise 3. hoopoe, hornbill bird, bee eater bird, secretary bird		A camel
20-21	1. grapes, oranges	2. cloves	A sand dune
22-23	1. Two. Germany and Belgium 2. Greece	3. Norway	
24-25	1. football, cricket, rugby 2. yachting, windsurfing 3. curling, skiing		A shamrock
26-27	1. Gouda 3. croissant	2. dairy cows, pigs, sheep	An owl
28-29			Spaghetti
30-31	Sri Lanka		
32-33	1. reindeer, polar bear, Siberian tiger, Siberian husky, Siberian stag, brown bear, lynx, Caspian seal, lemming 2. eider duck, snow goose, Ural owl		A brown bear
34-35	1. Arabian camel, Arabian fox, Arabian horse 2. Mosque	3. cricket	A flamingo
36-37	1. tiger, snow leopard, Asiatic lion 2. peacock, parakeet	3. Indian porcupine	An octopus
38-39	1. Giant panda 2. karate, sumo wrestling, skiing		A terracotta soldier
40-41	1. surfing and scuba diving		A Komodo dragon
42-43	FIJI AUSTRALIA NAURU		
44-45	1. black swan 2. sea horses, sperm whale, barracuda, flying fish, clown fish, great white shark, swordfish, octopus		A kangaroo
46	1. ski plane 3. snowmobile	2. kayak	
47			A penguin

63

Answers

56-57   Games and quizzes

Name the continents
1. North America
2. Europe
3. Asia
4. South America
5. Africa
6. Oceania
7. Antarctica

Name the countries
1. United States of America
2. Italy
3. Australia
4. Brazil
5. Thailand
6. France

Search for cities

A	O	W	E	L	L	I	N	G	T	O	N
B	P	X	Z	P	O	J	X	Z	Q	J	O
W	A	S	H	I	N	G	T	O	N	V	T
X	R	K	Y	Y	D	W	V	J	F	X	T
C	I	K	P	F	O	X	Z	Q	J	F	A
A	S	Z	B	A	N	G	K	O	K	X	W
N	J	V	Q	Z	X	X	C	H	Z	Y	A
B	R	A	S	I	L	I	A	W	X	T	V
E	W	H	G	M	X	Z	I	Z	F	U	X
R	O	M	E	X	Q	V	R	J	Q	N	F
R	V	W	T	O	K	Y	O	V	W	I	Q
A	Q	W	H	G	M	X	T	J	V	S	Q

Quiz 1
1. Russian Federation
2. Paris
3. 5 stars

Colour match
1. purple finch
2. pink flamingo
3. brown bear
4. blueberries
5. great white shark

Unscramble the countries
1. Japan
2. Italy
3. France
4. Mexico
5. India
6. Sudan

Quiz 2
1. River Nile
2. 3 (green, white and red)
3. Polar bears

Whose flag is this?
1. Canada
2. Australia
3. Greece
4. United States of America
5. Pakistan
6. Sweden
7. Brazil
8. Kenya
9. China
10. United Kingdom
11. New Zealand
12. Japan
13. Nepal
14. Chile
15. Republic of South Africa
16. Somalia

58-59   Games and quizzes

Name the oceans
1. Pacific Ocean
2. Atlantic Ocean
3. Indian Ocean
4. Arctic Ocean
5. Southern Ocean

Name the symbol
1. Puffin
2. Kiwi fruit
3. Walrus
4. Sydney Opera House
5. Cricket
6. Stonehenge

Quiz 3
1. Buenos Aires
2. 2
3. Japan

Symbol match
1. United Kingdom
2. France
3. United States of America
4. India
5. Australia
6. Swaziland

Which continent are you in?
1. Europe
2. Africa
3. North America
4. Asia
5. Oceania
6. South America

Search for countries

A	R	G	E	N	T	I	N	A	F	K	Y
N	V	G	F	Y	N	E	Z	U	Z	B	V
C	Y	D	Q	C	G	G	G	S	X	Q	J
H	U	N	G	A	R	Y	B	T	G	B	J
I	L	A	F	N	G	P	H	R	B	O	Q
N	N	L	Z	A	S	T	V	A	P	T	X
A	G	O	X	D	T	V	F	L	H	S	F
H	P	O	L	A	N	D	Z	I	H	W	F
H	Y	X	Q	Q	V	Z	X	A	Z	A	O
M	E	X	I	C	O	G	G	V	G	N	Q
Q	Z	J	B	Y	F	F	B	X	B	A	J
N	I	G	E	R	I	A	B	J	Q	K	P

Quiz 4
1. Mount Everest
2. Beijing
3. Australia

64